Princeton Theological Monograph Series

Dikran Y. Hadidian

General Editor

43

THE TRIAL OF JESUS CONTINUES

Rudolf Pesch

THE TRIAL OF JESUS CONTINUES

Translated from the German by

Doris Glenn Wagner

PICKWICK PUBLICATIONS
Allison Park, Pennsylvania

Published by

Pickwick Publications
4137 Timberlane Drive
Allison Park, PA 15101-2932
USA

Library of Congress Cataloging-in-Publication Data

Pesch, Rudolf, 1936-
    {Der prozess Jesu geht weiter. English}
    The trial of Jesus continues / Rudolf Pesch ; translated from the German by Doris Glenn Wagner
        p.   cm. -- (Princeton theological monograph series ; 43)
    ISBN 1-55635-033-3
    1. Jesus Christ--Trial.   I. Title.   II. Series.
BT440.P4713   1996
232.96'2--dc21
                                                                    96-47382
                                                                    CIP

CONTENTS

Part Two

THEOLOGICAL INSIGHTS

PREFACE

Whoever wants to pass judgment on the trial of Jesus will have to change her or his way of thinking. Whoever thinks that the issue was, in any case, a remote affair will not be concerned with it. Blaise Pascal noted in his *Pensées:* "Jesus Christ was in such darkness (corresponding to what the world calls darkness) that the historians who described only the most important affairs of state hardly noticed him." The New Testament tradition, the accounts of the gospels, tried to illuminate the darkness engulfing the Messiah. With the light of the Enlightenment, the modern age believed it could see more. It did see more, but also obscured more when it ignored the fact that in scripture a long process of God's enlightenment had taken place.

The trial of Jesus continues. Anyone can come forward as a witness—without risking her or his neck, and here in the "free West" without even a scratch. Our generation today participates in the decision regarding whether Jesus was a seducer or a rebel. Of course, this decision is not made in books, but books can nevertheless draw one's attention to it. Therefore I have written this small book.

Munich, October 1987

When after nine years I read my booklet again in the English translation, which makes it available to a new and wider public, I felt that the insights and thoughts presented in it are as valuable and actual as then, when I edited it first. I hope that it will make some readers reflect more about this theme—as it did before.

Rudolf Pesch

INTRODUCTION

Since the founding of the state of Israel on May 14, 1948, repeated attempts have been made to again bring the trial of Jesus before an Israeli court.

When the legal process was taken up after more than 1900 years, many Christians shared the expectation that the present Israeli judicial system, as descendent of the ancient Jewish Sanhedrin, would revise the earlier "false verdict" pronounced on Jesus as a seducer and thereby also prove false the judgment of the Roman prefect of that time about Jesus as rebel. In the spring of 1949, a Dutch lawyer, under the pseudonym of H. 187, reportedly made a formal petition with the Israeli justice department requesting a revision; and in 1972 Christian theologians reportedly filed a new petition with the supreme court of Israel requesting that the earlier sentence against Jesus be annulled. Israel's justice department declared that it was not the responsible authority to deal with the matter and referred the petitioners to an Italian court—an Italian court since, from the Jewish perspective, the Romans had sentenced and executed Jesus!

Almost annually during Lent journalists track down historians or theologians or lawyers who attempt to bring new-old hypotheses about the trial of Jesus before the public. In 1987 the notion once again came to the fore that Jesus was not sentenced by the Jews at all, but was rather executed by the Romans according to martial law. A Jewish proponent of this view considered his "Jewishness" a bonus with regard to the plausibility of his argument; a lawyer looked upon his being a lawyer as a bonus. Who is the proper authority? Which court? And what accountability is being sought? That of the lawyer, of the historian, of the

theologian? Of all of them together? Or, first of all, that of
the Christian church, which already as the primitive church,
a few weeks after Jesus' death, reopened the trial of Jesus
through their very existence and their preaching in Jerusalem—not judicially, but in the praxis of their daily lives
and theologically.

What is really at stake in Jesus' trial?

Our small book should primarily serve as a reflection on this question. The main key to answering this question is found in the liturgy of the church, which on Good
Friday, following the veneration of the cross in the *Impro-
peria*, voices the lament of God, or rather that of God's
Son, the Messiah, against God's people: "My people, what
have I done to you? How have I saddened you? Answer
me." The lament climaxes in the statement: "I raised you
high by great power—and you hung me high on the gallows!" The people of God addressed in the Good Friday liturgy is the gathered church, the "true Israel," the congregation of "God's enemies" who were saved and reconciled by
Jesus Christ and of whom Paul wrote in the letter to the Romans:

> "We were reconciled with God through the
> death of his son while we were still enemies of
> God." (Romans 5:10).

The people of God addressed by God, that is, the
church, cannot put their responsibility for what is at stake
in the trial of Jesus onto "the Jews" of Jesus' day, and surely not onto "Judaism" as such, but also not, within Judaism,
onto the Sadducees or, outside it, onto the Romans. The
historical examination of the development of the trial
against Jesus of Nazareth, before the Sanhedrin and before
the court of the prefect Pontius Pilate, and the legal examination of the legitimacy or illegitimacy of the trial can only
serve to elicit the more comprehensive theological dimension of this trial, in which "church and state," the highest
Jewish religious officials and the representative of the Roman emperor, were involved, namely, the question of truth,

God's truth and human truth and the question of the historical verification of God's rule among God's people and of
their form of life. What was at stake, when, after the long
history of Israel from the time of Abraham, the Messiah
had come in Jesus of Nazareth? The question posed by the
trial of Jesus can—in view of its universal significance with
respect to salvation history—be articulated in very many
ways. Following the historical and legal-historical examination, we shall trace, first of all, the canonical gospel accounts before we attempt, with the help of John's Gospel,
to articulate an interpretation presented to us by the historical moment *today*. The reader is then presented two parts: a
historical examination and theological insights.

Because I have for several years presented my insights in generally understandable paperback form, I have
occasionally received criticism from academic circles. I
was encouraged to continue by one of the most enlightened
thinkers who stood at the beginning of the development of
the historical-critical method and—because it came by way
of experience—already anticipated many things; I mean the
aphorist Georg Christoph Lichtenberg, who wrote two hundred years ago in his oilcloth notebook:

> "Chained to the university slave ships"—
> "Our theologians want to force the Bible to be a
>   book void of human reason"—
> "Most teachers of Christianity defend their sen-
>   tences not because they themselves are con-
>   vinced of their truth, but rather because they
>   once asserted their truth" —
> "Books are written from books . . ."

PART ONE

HISTORICAL EXAMINATION

I

WHAT DO WE KNOW ABOUT THE TRIAL OF JESUS?

What Do We Know about the Trial of Jesus?

Jesus of Nazareth was—according to the more probable chronology—put to death on Friday, April 7, 30 A.D., on the place called "the Skull" outside of Jerusalem's city walls; he was hanged high on a cross, nailed to it, and after a few hours he died.

According to all four canonical gospels—Matthew, Mark, Luke, and John—which agree on this point, as well as to the apocryphal Gospel of Peter, the *titulus crucis*, that is, the title of accusation, nailed on the cross by the soldiers of the Roman procurator Pontius Pilate who made up the execution commando and acted on behalf of the provincial Roman governor and the supreme judge, said: "King of the Jews."

This made the *causa poenae*, the cause for the punishment and the reason for execution, public. Jesus of Nazareth was marked as a rebel, as a political criminal, as a perpetrator of high treason. Corresponding to this condemnation was his crucifixion between two "robbers," two political rebels, who were probably radical freedom fighters or revolutionary bandits.

How did it come to this? Why was Jesus condemned to death? Why was he punished by the dishonorable and cruel execution on the cross? Who was responsible for his execution? What do we know about Jesus' trial?

This question is not answered unanimously in the gospels, as we might have expected in light of the gospels' agreement regarding the *titulus crucis*. With regard to their information on the development of Jesus' trial and their statements with respect to those primarily responsible for Jesus' death, the gospels differ not inconsiderably from each other. A well-founded, responsible contemporary interpretation of Jesus' trial must deal with these facts. And, first of all, this state of affairs must be recognized.

Let us, then, first orient ourselves sufficiently by considering the most important statements of the gospel accounts which differ from each other.

The Different Accounts of the Gospels

If one wanted to look at all of the ways in which the gospels differ from each other, with regard to the course taken by Jesus' trial, one would be obliged to present a rather long list or treatise. The reader interested in a more exact study can make him—or herself such a detailed overview by utilizing a gospel synopsis. We shall limit ourselves here to the most important points. They concern:

The Arrest of Jesus by Jews and/or Romans

According to the evangelists Matthew and Mark, the troop arresting Jesus, which was led to the Mount of Olives by Judas Iscariot, was "a crowd armed with swords and clubs, from the chief priests, the scribes and the elders"; according to Luke, also "the chief priests and officers of the temple and the elders" belonged to this group. John named, finally, "a detachment of soldiers" *(speira)* and "police from the chief priests and the Pharisees." The fourth evangelist raises herewith the question of whether also a commando, a cohort, of Roman soldiers already, participated in the arrest of Jesus, which was instigated by Judas on the night of the Passover in the garden of Gethsemane. The Gospel of John speaks at the end of its arrest scene of "the soldiers, their officer and the Jewish police" and thus appears also to hint that the cohort of soldiers was not Jews.

The Deliverance of Jesus to Caiaphas or, first, to Annas,
  the Father-in-Law of the High Priest

According to the account in the Gospel of Mark, after his arrest Jesus "was taken to the high priest"; undoubtedly, Caiaphas, whom the evangelist Matthew then also expressly names, is here intended. Luke writes of the deliverance of Jesus "to the high priest's house." Again, the Fourth Gospel differs markedly from the others: "First they took him to Annas, who was the father-in-law of Caiaphas, the high priest that year." If the following descriptions of the interrogation before the Sanhedrin, and respectively the hearing of Jesus before Annas, were not likewise so different from each other, one could overlook these inconsistencies. However, as it is, the question remains important: Was Jesus taken first to Annas or immediately to Caiaphas?

The Time of the Sanhedrin Interrogation.
Still during the Night or only Next Morning?
The Place: In the House of the High Priest or in the
  Official Building of the Council?

According to the account in the Gospel of Mark, which Matthew follows, the Sanhedrin interrogation, the judicial session of the supreme council, begins immediately with the high priest. At the home of the high priest "all the chief priests, the elders, and the scribes were assembled." Mark describes the beginning of the interrogation thus:

"Now the chief priests and the whole council were looking for testimony against Jesus to put him to death." According to the Lukan report, on the other hand, "the assembly of the elders of the people, both chief priests and scribes, gathered together" only "when the day came"; they deliberated early in the morning, however, not in the house of the high priest, but they rather led Jesus away "to their Sanhedrin," to their meeting place in their official building.

In the Gospel of John, Jesus was, in any case, not immediately brought to Caiaphas, but rather, first of all, to his father-in-law Annas. Jesus was questioned by Annas

"about his disciples and about his teaching" before Annas
"sent him bound to Caiaphas, the high priest." In the Fourth
Gospel, an interrogation in the Sanhedrin, during the night
or on the morrow, is not mentioned at all. After the denial
of Peter has been related in two parts, it immediately says:
"Then they took Jesus from Caiaphas to the praetorium,"
that is, to Pontius Pilate's headquarters. What happened to
Jesus while he was with Caiaphas is not made known to the
reader.

On this third point, therefore, not only did the first
three gospels, the so-called synoptics, differ from the
Fourth Gospel, John, but here the third evangelist Luke also
clearly differs from the first two. In the Lukan account of
the trial, the legal session against Jesus takes place only in
the morning and at a different place, namely, in the meeting
hall of the supreme council.

Did an Interrogation Before the Sanhedrin Take Place at All? And What Course Did It Take?

In the accounts of Mark and Matthew we learn the
following about the Sanhedrin interrogations which took
place during the night: First, false witnesses against Jesus
come forward, "and their testimony did not agree." Then,
additional witnesses come forward who quote a saying of
Jesus allegedly aimed against the temple; their evidence,
however, as further elaborated, "did not agree" (and was
therewith, according to the Jewish law, unacceptable as
proof). Jesus is silent before the accusations of the witnesses. Only when the question of his being the Messiah is
raised by the high priest does he answer: "I am," or—
according to Matthew—"You have said so." Jesus then
threatens his judges with the judgment of the Son of Man.
This is considered blasphemy and leads to his sentence, "he
deserves death."

During the morning interrogation of the Sanhedrin
as described by Luke, no witnesses come forward at all;
rather, the assembly—as in chorus—asks the question

about his being the Messiah, which Jesus does not answer, and then the question: "Are you, then, the Son of God?" Jesus answers: "You say that I am!" At this point, his interrogators realize that they need no further proof. There is, however, no talk of a formal sentencing by the supreme council, though the fact that he admitted to being God's Son, a crime felt to be worthy of death, can be considered an accusation.

Missing in the Fourth Gospel, as already mentioned, is an account of the Sanhedrin interrogation during the night or on the morning following Jesus' arrest. Therefore, also the question of whether such a meeting ever took place at all is a pressing one.

The Time and Manner in Which Jesus Was Handed Over to Pilate

According to the accounts in the Gospels of Mark and Matthew, Jesus was handed over to Pilate "as soon as it was morning," after the Sanhedrin had "held a consultation." Matthew says that it had "conferred together against Jesus in order to bring about his death." According to Luke, Jesus was brought before Pilate following the morning session of the council of elders. The final scene in the official meeting hall is described thus: "Then the assembly rose as a body and brought Jesus before Pilate." In the Johannine account, Jesus was, as we have already heard, led "from Caiaphas to the praetorium." The Johannine report continues: "It was early in the morning"; and this information is consistent with Matthew and Mark, though in the latter accounts the nocturnal Sanhedrin interrogation precedes the meeting with Pilate.

The Dating of the Day of Jesus' death. Friday, the 14th or 15th of Nisan, the Day of Preparation or the Day of the Passover Feast?

Though on the morning when Jesus was handed

over to Pilate we find ourselves, according to the chronology of the first three evangelists, on the day of the Passover
Feast, on the 15th of Nisan (the month of spring of the Jewish calendar) John knows this Friday, the day before the
Sabbath, as the day of Preparation, the 14th of Nisan. For
John speaks of the Jewish officials who delivered Jesus up
to Pilate thus: "They themselves did not enter the praetorium, so as to avoid [by mixing with Gentiles in the house of
the Gentile governor] ritual defilement and to be able to eat
the Passover." According to the description of the first
three gospels, Jesus had already, in the night before his arrest, taken the Passover meal with his disciples in Jerusalem.

The Course Taken by the Trial before Pilate

All four evangelists agree that, before Pilate, Jesus
was accused by the Jewish leadership of pretending to be
the Messiah, of being a political rebel and of committing
high treason. Since Pilate asks the accused: "You are the
King of the Jews?", he presupposes that that is the charge.
While Mark and Matthew report on the surprise of the Roman prefect at the silence of Jesus before the accusations of
the Jewish leadership, Luke and John say that Pontius Pilate explicitly stated Jesus' innocence three times. The
fourth evangelist describes a detailed interrogation of Jesus
by the Roman prefect and a public confrontation between
this Roman and the Jewish accusers of the Jew Jesus.

The Reasons Why Jesus was Condemned to the Cross

According to the accounts of Mark and Matthew,
Jesus is finally crucified because Pilate "wished to satisfy
the crowd," which demands the release of Barabbas and the
crucifixion of Jesus. According to Luke, "Pilate delivered
Jesus up to their will" (i.e., did according to the Jews' wish-
es). John likewise reports this.
According to the account of the third evangelist

Luke, Pilate considered Jesus innocent and, against his convictions, submitted to the cries for crucifixion coming from the masses; according to the presentation of the fourth evangelist John, the Roman prefect was finally put under pressure by the Jewish leaders, when they threatened him, and allowed him to be threatened, by claiming that he was no longer a "friend of the emperor" if he pardoned a "King of the Jews," an enemy of the emperor, and allowed him to live and go free.

The *inconsistencies* of the four gospels in their accounts of Jesus' trial are then considerable; the eight more important points, which we have briefly discussed, render understandable the fact that different scholars have given different information with respect to the course taken by Jesus' trial and that very different conclusions have been drawn—depending on which source material has been primarily drawn upon and how different sources have been combined, and depending on how important legal-historical facts and dates have been interpreted.

Three Directions of Historical Valuation

While traditionally Jews and Romans have been considered responsible for the execution of Jesus to different degrees, there were and are voices which consider the Roman governor alone responsible and—as, for example, the Jewish judge and legal historian, H. Cohn—even think that the high priest did not want to kill Jesus, but rather tried to save him. Finally, there are also voices which put all reponsibility on the shoulders of the Jewish officials in Jerusalem at that time. One can summarize the three directions opinion has taken in the following headings:

1. Jews and Romans,
2. the Roman governor alone,
3. the Jewish officials alone.

If in the first case one thinks most often of a double

trial (before the Sanhedrin and before Pilate) with different accusations (blasphemy or high treason—that is, before the Great Jewish Council, what counted was what was interpreted as Jesus' presumed claim to be the Messiah and the Son of God, which was considered blasphemy; before the Roman governor, the evidence for political high treason, which could be derived from the Messiah claim), in the second case, it is insinuated that Jesus appeared on the scene, or rather was misunderstood, as a political revolutionary and was arrested by the Roman occupation army; and, finally, in the third case, that Jesus was handed over and sentenced by the Jewish court officials as a false teacher and a seducer of the people.

Which Direction Can One Follow with Good Reasons?

Since for all three directions one can to some degree appeal to the gospels as sources, or at least to a combination of gospel data and historico-judicial information, it is difficult for the layperson to know how to approach the issue, given such a variety of opinions with such varying valuations regarding Jesus' trial. Are there possibilities for guidance?

The different appeal to the various interpretations of the different gospels can, first of all, be narrowed only by defining the sources more exactly according to age and the value of the witness, therewith clarifying in a more reliable manner the condition out of which the question arose regarding the course taken by Jesus' trial. We cannot trace here the process of such clarification, but rather only offer its results, since one is dealing with the question of the relationship of the four gospels to each other, of the interdependence of the different gospels or their independence from each other, a question which has in the meantime been dealt with for hundreds of years. In addition to this, one is concerned with the question of the older sources upon which the accounts of the gospels are based (and which even in an earlier gospel could be older and, in certain cases, more reliable). And scholars are in no way agreed regarding this complex and complicated problem. At this point we shall mention only the main controversial points which touch upon the trial of Jesus.

Controversial Valuations Regarding the State of the Sources

According to the two-source theory, the most widely known theory and the one advocated by the majority of New Testament scholars, Mark's Gospel is the oldest source, on which Matthew's and Luke's Gospels—independent from each other—are dependent. On the foundation of this theory, we can consider it accepted that Matthew's account of the passion, and particularly the trial of Jesus, is a redactional treatment of Mark's material. Apart from the name of the officiating high priest, Caiaphas, and the assessment of Jesus by his opponents as *planos* (impostor), as false teacher and seducer of the people, Matthew's Gospel offers no original and reliable information. Controversial, on the other hand, also among representatives of the two-source theory, is still the question whether, in its account of the passion and the trial of Jesus, the Third Gospel, the Gospel of Luke, used *only* the Markan material or, additionally, also a special source which offered original (and reliable) information going beyond the sources utilized by Mark. And whether this special source knew, for example, about the meeting of the supreme council in the Sanhedrin, in the official building, early in the morning and thus guarantees its historicity, especially since a night meeting of the council would have been, according to valid law of that time, improper? Was this source also aware of the presentation of Jesus to King Herod Antipas, the provincial Galilean prince to whom Pilate sent his accused, since the latter came from his area?

Likewise controversial is the question of whether John's account, the youngest, which differs most from the remaining three reports, deserves to be trusted at all with respect to its historic reliability, or whether it still in fact preserves information from old Palestinian tradition which, though opposing the accounts of the synoptics, may be trusted. Is John correct in saying that Jesus was executed already on the 14th of Nisan, on the day of Preparation? Is the dating based on historical knowledge as reliable as is the reference to the *ius gladii,* which was reserved for the Roman prefect? The Jews did maintain in the Fourth Gospel, before the court of Pilate: "We are not permitted to put anyone to death" (John 18:31).

A Defensible Position

The interpretation here represented, which I have substantiated in numerous studies and which I myself consider quite probable, allows a partially new judgment about the particularities of Jesus' trial. I have tried, in the pertinent works (named in the note below[1]), to show:

---

1. Cf. R. Pesch, *So liest man synoptisch. Anleitung und Kommentar zum Studium der synoptischen Evangelien,* vols. I-VII (Frankfurt a.M. 1975-1980); *Das Markusevangelium,* vols. I-II (Herders Theologischer Kommentar zum Neuen Testament II,1-2; Freiburg i.Br. 1976-1977, 5,1989, 4,1991); "Die Uberlieferung des Passion Jesu" in: K. Kertelge, ed., *Rückfrage nach Jesus* (Quaestiones Disputatae 63; Freiburg i.Br. 1974) 148-173; "Die Passion des Menschensohnes. Eine Studie zu den Menschensohnworten der vormarkinischen Passionsgeschichte" in: *Jesus und der Menschensohn. Festschrift für A. Vögtle* (Freiburg i.Br. 1975) 166-195; *Das Abendmahl und Jesu Todesverständnis* (Quaestiones Disputate 80; Freiburg i.Br. 1978); *Die Johannes-Synopse. Ergänzungsband zum Synoptischen Arbeitsbuch* (Gütersloh-Zürich 1981); "Das Evangelium in Jerusalem. Mk 14,12-26 als ältestes Überlieferungsgut der Urgemeinde" in: P. Stuhlmacher, ed., *Das Evangelium und die Evangelien* (Wissenschaftliche Untersuchungen zum Neuen Testament 28; Tübingen 1983) 113-155; English trans.: "The Gospel in Jerusalem: Mark 14:12-26 as the Oldest Tradition of the Early Church", in: P. Stuhlmacher, ed., *The Gospel and the Gospels* (Grand Rapids, Mich. 1991) 106-148.

1. The Markan Passion narrative with its account of Jesus' trial, which appears in the Gospel of Mark, is largely identical with the pre-Markan passion narrative, upon which the evangelist drew; in the passages from the arrest to the crucifixion of Jesus, the two are virtually the same. The pre-Markan Passion narrative, about which I wrote in the small monograph *Evangelium der Urgemeinde* (Herder-bücherei No.748), was, in my opinion, already born and formulated, in the primitive church in Jerusalem, during the first six or seven years following Jesus' execution. It is the oldest source we can draw upon for a reconstruction of Jesus' trial.

2. Luke's presentation, which is dependent on Mark's material, is throughout a redactional treatment of Markan material, presupposing no additional, original, special source and probably not even a single special tradition. In judging the Lukan Passion narrative, one must rather take into account that traditional material of Luke's second book, the Acts of the Apostles, influenced the redaction of the material of the first book. Luke learned, for example, from the trial reports of the Acts of the Apostles, that occasionally Sanhedrin interrogations took place, or were meant to take place, early in the morning.

3. John's presentation is at essential points—for example, its chronology which places Jesus' day of death one day earlier—secondary compared to the pre-Markan account; it can, therefore, not be consulted as a whole, but rather only in its particulars, to supplement our reconstruction of the trial of Jesus. The reconstruction must, first of all, build upon the foundation of the pre-Markan account.

New Studies

A reconstruction of Jesus' trial, based on the ancient Passion narrative from the primitive church of Jerusalem, can orient itself by means of several studies which appeared successively at the beginning of the 1980s and led, to a certain extent, to astounding convergences. I mention:

1. The small study of French lawyer Jean Imbert, *Le procès de Jèsus* (Que sais je?) (Paris, 1980). From Jean Imbert can one learn, for example, that no Roman cohort had to have taken part in the arrest of Jesus, since the vocabulary (*speira, chiliarchos*) used by Luke and John is documented in the Greek translation of the Old Testament and does not necessarily point to the Roman army (cf. pp. 21f.). Jean Imbert confirms that, at the time of Jesus, the Sanhedrin did not have the authority over capital punishment, that is, could not execute a death sentence (cf. p. 36). He confirms moreover that the custom of amnesty on the Passover, which reportedly corresponds to Roman law and Jewish practice, need not be skeptically viewed as unhistorical (cf. pp. 77f.).

2. The major study of Protestant New Testament scholar August Strobel, *Die Stunde der Wahrheit. Untersuchungen zum Strafverfahren gegen Jesus* (Wissenschaftliche Untersuchungen zum Neuen Testament 21; Tübingen 1980).

Strobel carefully traces once again particularly the legal-historical questions by using early Jewish sources and considers some of the details of the Markan account highly probable. However, his view—due to the different valuation of sources—differs from ours in a number of respects.

3. Likewise the major study of French exegete Jean-Pierre Lemonon, *Pilate et le Gouvernement de la Judée. Textes et Monuments* (Études Bibliques; Paris 1981). This study contributes to the clarification of the role of the Roman prefect, Pontius Pilate, in the trial of Jesus and comes to the same conclusions of the other studies which we shall summarize in a moment.

4. The work of Columbian New Testament scholar Hernando Guevara, *La Resistencia Judia contra Roma en la Época de Jesús* (Meitingen 1981).

This study attempts to prove that the Romans did not believe Jesus to be, and did not sentence Jesus specifically as, a "zealot"=anti-Roman freedom-fighter. The term "zealot" was used to document violent opposition to Rome only from the beginning of the Jewish war (66 A.D.) and thereafter.

5. The major monograph of Protestant New Testament scholar and scholar of Jewish studies Otto Betz, *Probleme des Prozesses Jesu*, in: H. Temporini / W. Haase, eds., *Aufstieg und Niedergang der römischen Welt. II. Prinzipat* (vol. 25, I; Berlin 1982) pp. 565-647. Betz once again reviews—as did Strobel—the Jewish sources, primarily also the pertinent passages in the temple scroll from Qumran, which make the case against Jesus as an exceptional case against the "seducer" understandable.

A New Consensus

In view of lengthy controversies, the consensus which becomes visible in the more recent studies of important questions is of greatest significance. We shall, first, draw special attention to three groups of questions.

1. Regarding the question of the *ius gladii*, "the right of the sword", of capital punishment, in the Roman province of Judea at that time, the view is confirmed that the Jewish Sanhedrin could indeed pronounce death sentences but could not carry them out. Capital punishment had been handed over from the Herodians (Herod the Great and subsequently his son Archelaus) to the Roman procurators and was situated then in the court of Pilate, to whom the Jewish leaders had to turn if they wanted to pursue the execution of Jesus.

2. Regarding the question of the *privilegium paschale*, of the Easter amnesty customary in Jerusalem under the Roman procurators, the view is confirmed that a practice, which is reported on by the gospels in the context of the Barabbas episode, is no legendary creation of the narrator of the Passion tradition, but can rather be understood as a historical fact in the course of Jesus' trial.

3. Regarding the question of the most reliable source, the Markan account of the trial (and thereby, in our opinion, the account of the ancient pre-Markan Passion nar-

rative) corresponds essentially to the historical chain of events as they happened, i.e., to actual happenings, not withstanding its kerygmatic and historico-theological interpretation of the happenings. The interpretative account of the gospel comprehends—of course, above the level of factual happenings and in a first attempt—the deep dimension of salvation history.

Clarification of Legal-Historical Questions

The studies of August Strobel and Otto Betz contribute, not only to the consensus just described, but also to the clarification of important legal-historical questions; for a long time, deviations of the ancient Passion narrative from the legal tradition of the Jewish Mishna, with which we are familiar, have been used to question the faithfulness of Christian transmitters of tradition to that tradition and to argue against the historicity of their accounts. Such deviations concern primarily the following three issues:

1. According to valid Jewish laws, criminal cases had to be handled and decided *during the day*. The *nocturnal meeting* of the Sanhedrin, described in Mark's Gospel (and, following him, Matthew) would subsequently have been illegal. Repeatedly, therefore, one has wanted to conclude that the meeting cannot have taken place as described.

2. Between the time the evidence was received and the sentence was passed, the Jewish court should have *allowed one day to pass*, in order to avoid a legal error in criminal cases and protect the accused. Since, according to the accounts of all Passion narratives, Jesus was *sentenced and executed on the same day*, the court would have acted unlawfully. Also from this, one wanted to conclude that the trial of Jesus cannot have happened as the tradition of the early church describes it.

3. According to Jewish law, no sentence could be passed on the day of Preparation to the Sabbath. Friday

could, subsequently, not have been a trial day.

All of these arguments, which were derived from the Jewish legal tradition and speak against the probability of the course of events of Jesus' trial as portrayed in the oldest gospel, insinuate, of course, that nothing would ever happen which is forbidden by law. The world, our history, is full of transgressions against laws! If one wanted to make valid laws the measuring rod for the reconstruction of actual history, then one would, at every turn, be led astray.

In our special case, however, we should now, according to August Strobel and Otto Betz whose work is based on an examination of Jewish sources, reflect on the following:

For the case of the *seducer*, the false prophet, who—as codified in the Torah in the book of Deuteronomy, chapters 13 and 17—speaks "treason against the Lord your God" (Deut 13:5), there are *special regulations* operative in Jewish law which are exceptions to general punitive legal processes, since the case of the seducer is, in early Judaism, also a case of "explosive civil danger" (A. Strobel, p. 7). Jesus' attack on the temple and his teaching regarding the temple labeled him, in the eyes of the Sadducee leadership, the circle around the high priest in Jerusalem, as a "seducer," who in accordance with Deut 13 and 17 should be rigorously opposed—and precisely by the Jewish leadership who should take care of those "things given by God: the people, the temple and the Holy City" (O. Betz, p. 600).

According to contemporary interpretation of Deut 21:22f., which has now been substantiated by the temple scroll from Qumran, a *seducer* who misleads and slanders God's people and "betrays his people to a foreign nation" —as the account in the Gospel of John describes Caiphas's judgment of Jesus!—should be hanged on the cross, that is, crucified! Crucified should be also, according to the interpretation of Deut 21:22f., blasphemers against God; the Old Testament expression, that the crucified are "God's curse," was interpreted as *genitivus subjectivus*, "They are cursed by God," and as *genitivus objectivus*, "They have cursed

God."

According to the Passion tradition of the gospels, Jesus was sentenced by the High Council as a blasphemer; he was considered by the Jewish leadership to be *a seducer*. In his case, Jewish law had exceptional regulations for exceptional legal proceedings, which we shall later consider more closely when we reconstruct Jesus' trial.

What Do We Know about Jesus' Trial? More than Before!

We can, first of all, state that both new sources, primarily the temple scroll from Qumran published only a few years ago, and new studies allow us today to say to the question of what we know about Jesus' trial: More than before! We are in a position to make a new attempt to reconstruct the event.

We are, however, also in a position to do greater justice to the interpretation of the event, which the four evangelists undertook in different ways, particularly the theologically most intensive interpretation of the fourth evangelist. And we can finally ask more precisely how each respective interpretation, which from the theological perspective is viewed through the eyes of God, corresponds to history. Israel, the people of God, practiced seeing "with the eyes of God" over a long learning process; it learned that the new way of seeing is a gift, a blessing. To interpret history and to narrate it interpretively has remained the supreme task of theology.

We shall narrate history, first of all, as it appears to the historian, as it is deduced from our reconstruction based on the oldest source, the pre-Markan Passion narrative—with the help of all insights which the more recent studies have made possible.

Of course, the oldest source leaves many questions open which we can ask ourselves but for which we find no answer, at least no sure answer. Who were the informants of the narrators of the primitive church? What did the community really learn about what took place in the house of the high priest? Was Joseph of Arimathea or Nicodemus an informant? Was the information which trickled down to the early church from accounts given by members of the Sanhedrin fairly exact or only general? Did the disciples of Jesus imagine or reconstruct the main accusation and the presumed arguments of Jesus on the basis of rather vague clues?

There is no possible way to answer such questions indisputably. Whoever prefers to doubt, rather than trust, the reliability of tradition will be more reticent in their judgment. We present here a reconstruction which rather trusts tradition, if justified doubts can be convincingly eliminated. We narrate the course of events of Jesus' trial with this presupposition.

II

THE COURSE TAKEN BY JESUS' TRIAL

From Jesus' Entry into Jerusalem
to His Execution on the Cross

On Sunday

Jesus entered into Jerusalem *on the first day of the week*, the Sunday before the Passover Feast, presumably on the 2nd of April, 30 A.D., coming from Jericho at the head of an enthusiastic messianic group of his disciples and followers and additional Galilean feast day pilgrims, who had been witnesses in Jericho to the healing of blind Bartimaeus. According to the oldest account, Jesus was celebrated as the "One coming in the name of JHWH"; that was, admittedly, no open homage to the Messiah, since the Psalm passage fits every feast-day pilgrim; however, the addition, "Blessed be the kingdom of our ancestor David," clearly alluded to messianic expectations. It cannot be doubted that the Jewish leaders in Jerusalem, who certainly were more afraid than the Roman governor of unrest on a major feast day, were aroused by such a demonstration.

On Monday

On the following second day of the Week, Monday, probably the 3rd of April, 30 A.D., Jesus had demonstrated in the temple with a symbolic, prophetic action for the renewal and gathering of Israel in an eschatologically reformed temple community. The outer courtyard of the Gentiles should not, as already the prophet Jeremiah had lamented, be made a "den of robbers," but rather, as the prophet Isaiah had proclaimed in a saying of "the Lord God who gathers the outcasts of Israel," the house of prayer for all Gentile nations. Jesus' prophetic action in the outer courtyard of the Gentiles, a small part of the huge temple area, was undoubtedly limited; neither the temple police nor the Roman soldiers patrolling the corridors around the temple yard intervened. But, by this, Jesus made opponents of Jerusalem's temple aristocracy: "And when the chief priests and the scribes heard it, they kept looking for a way to kill him; for they were afraid of him, because the whole crowd was spellbound by his teaching" (Mk 11:18).

On Tuesday

On the third day, Tuesday, the 4th of April, 30 A.D., there were two attempts to arrest Jesus, since he, after staying overnight in Bethany (where he, as guest of Galileans, was safe in the circle of Galilean followers), was again to be found around the temple. At first, a delegation of the Sanhedrin comes—in the old account it says "the chief priests, the scribes, and the elders"—and questions him about his authority: "By what authority are you doing these things? Who gave you this authority to do them?" (Mk 11:28). The question refers to the action of Jesus in the outer courtyard of the Gentiles on the previous day. The interrogators want to know whether Jesus presumes to have an authority which would, to their eyes and according to the yardstick of the law they interpreted, label him *seducer*. The interrogators probably expected Jesus, chiefly against the background of news about the entry of Jesus into Jerusalem two days before, to claim to be the Messiah, which would have allowed them to accuse and judge Jesus as false teacher and seducer and present him to the procurator Pontius Pilate as messianic pretender and, thereby, traitor. The procurator was just then, during the Passover feast days, personally present in Jerusalem, in order to fulfill his duty as protector of the temple (which Jesus appeared to attack); he could, precisely in this role, be called upon at short notice by the Jewish leadership. Pilate was normally in the capital city of Israel during feast times, in order to quell germs of anti-Roman unrest.

Jesus did not answer the authority question. He refused to answer because he himself had received no answer to his counter question regarding the authority of John the Baptist. The old account says: "Jesus said to them, 'I will ask you one question; answer me, and I will tell you by what authority I do these things. Did the baptism of John come from heaven, or was it of human origin? Answer me!'" The delegation of the Sanhedrin did not want to commit themselves, did not want to admit that John had acted in divine authority as prophet; however, they also did not want to label him as a self-appointed false teacher and seducer because John was looked upon by the people as a prophet of highest standing. Therefore, the delegation of the Sanhedrin gave no answer to Jesus' question and thus enabled him then to refuse to answer. That Jesus insinuated indirectly that his authority came "from heaven," that it was given by God, became, of course, clear.

With the parable of the wicked tenants, Jesus then immediately makes use of his prophetic authority by attacking his opponents as successors to the murderers of the prophets. He tells a story about rebellious farmers which, over and against the images he uses (vineyard=Israel; tenants=leaders of the people; the slaves of the landowner= the prophets, etc.), becomes increasingly transparent as a parable of the history of Israel. In the image of the murder of the son and inheritor, Jesus warns his opponents who would see him killed. Their reaction is given in Mk 12:12: "When they realized that he had told this parable against them, they wanted to arrest him, but they feared the crowd."

In the ancient account of the Jerusalem community about the happenings related to Jesus' action in the temple and his provocation with the parable of the tenants of the vineyard, there are perhaps shortened versions of what Jesus did and said during these days before the feast. The tradition certainly throws into relief the central points of conflict and desires to characterize, in summary fashion, the works of Jesus in Jerusalem; and it also probably does this correctly, as far as history is concerned, when it does not provide a protocol. An interpretive condensed version is, in light of the "matter" considered, "more exact." John's Gospel brings us closer to this insight, as we shall see. First, however, we shall return to the sequence of happenings as presented in the oldest account.

The second attempt "to catch Jesus with a word," is then undertaken by a delegation of Pharisees and Herodians (followers of the reigning tetrarch in Galilee, Herod Antipas): Jesus should give his opinion about the legality of the emperor's taxes and, thereby, either discredit himself in the eyes of the people, by showing himself a friend of the Romans, or deliver himself up to his opponents by recommending tax evasion. That the emperor had collected a poll-tax through his officials here, ever since Judea had become a Roman province in 6 A.D., had for the majority of Jews become an irritation, and for the zealots, an occasion for repeated revolt. If Jesus had expressed himself as opponent of the emperor's taxes in the manner of the zealot, then his opponents would have had—as the evangelist Luke correctly interpreted—a good reason "to hand him over to the jurisdiction and authority of the governor" (Lk 20:20). Luke later relates events as if the members of the Sanhedrin had accused Jesus against their better knowledge: "We found this man perverting our nation, forbidding us to pay taxes to the emperor" (Lk 23:2).

But Jesus, as the oldest account tells, brilliantly avoided the trap set for him and silenced his opponents. Jesus used their trick for his own purposes and asked that he be shown a tax coin with the image and inscription of the emperor. Whatever carries the imprint of the emperor, he explains, belongs evidently to the emperor and may be given back to him as tax. At the same time, however, Jesus pointed out to his opponents that, as an image of God, every person belongs to God: "Give to God the things that are God's!"

Both attempts, to accuse Jesus in public and to deduce incriminating evidence against him from his own words, failed. His opponents became increasingly embarrassed in the face of his growing popularity and the traditional excitement surrounding the approaching Passover Feast.

On Wednesday

On the following 4th day, Wednesday, the 5th of April, 30 A.D., Jesus did not come to Jerusalem to the temple. He remained in Bethany where he had usually, up to that time, spent the night. On this day he was a guest in the house of Simon the leper. Tradition tells how a woman lavishly anointed him.

In Jerusalem the chief priests and scribes plot "for a way to arrest Jesus by stealth and kill him" (Mk 14:1). They see no chance of arresting him during the feast-day gathering in the temple because they fear the arrest of the celebrated prophet and teacher in public would incite an uprising of the people. Proceeding "by stealth" was in the case of a seducer of the people, which is what the officials took Jesus for, also provided for according to the laws of the time, as August Strobel has proven with references to texts of the Tosephtha. TSanh VII,11 says: "For all who are guilty of the punishment of death (as named) by law, one may not set traps, except for the *seducer*." The fact that Jesus was labeled by the Jewish authorities as "seducer" is documented in both Matthew's and John's Gospels, but also sufficiently in Jewish tradition as it relates to Jesus' death. The oldest Passion narrative did not, therefore, simply characterize the proceedings of Jesus' opponents negatively, when it said that the chief priests and scribes had wanted to arrest Jesus "by stealth"; it rather correctly adhered to a significant legal-historical fact, a historical event in the process leading to the trial of Jesus.

Judas Iscariot assisted the authorities who had tried to set a "trap" for the seducer Jesus and offered to betray Jesus for "silver," that is, for a corresponding payment, whenever a good "opportunity" arose (Mk 14:11). The next good opportunity arose during Passover night, that is, after the events of the following day. Supposedly, Judas informed the authorities that he intended to use this opportunity and asked them to make all necessary preparations. Otherwise, one can hardly explain the smooth course taken by the proceedings against Jesus in the night of the Passover.

On Thursday

On the 5th Day, Thursday, the evening of the 14th of Nisan, the 6th of April, 30 A.D., Jesus came to Jerusalem to take the Passover Feast in the circle of his twelve disciples. Ancient tradition gives us hints that Jesus rightly judged the development which was threatening him. Jesus had agreed with a landlord in Jerusalem, who made the room in an upper chamber available to him for the Passover meal, to make a sign which made it possible for him to keep secret his presence in Jerusalem during the night of Passover. The two disciples who should prepare the meal were referred to a man with a water jug (which normally only women carried and which therefore was noticeable): they should follow him into the concern house. Presumably, apart from Jesus no one knew where he would take the Passover meal with the Twelve. Likewise according to ancient tradition, during the meal Jesus himself reportedly made dark hints about a threatening betrayal from among the inner circle around him: "One of you will betray me!" And, in addition to this, during the Passover meal, he explained at the outset the death which threatened him as the primitive church later interpreted it, namely, as the substitutionary atoning suffering of the messianic servant of God.

On Friday

Following the Passover meal, Jesus remained with the Twelve—as pious Jews were commanded to do—in the city of Jerusalem, where, during this night, the Garden of Gethsemane on the slope of the Mount of Olives was to be included. Judas must have learned where Jesus wanted to retire with his disciples, for he—presumably in the darkness of the narrow alleys of Jerusalem—stole away and ran to the chief priests, in order to use this good opportunity. Judas led the "crowd with swords and clubs," a Jewish police troop, which had been placed at his disposal by "the chief priests, the scribes, and the elders," to the Mount of Olives in the Garden of Gethsemane. In the protection of night this troop could now easily take action against Jesus, who was accompanied only by the eleven apostles; the larger mass of Jesus' Galilean followers learned what had happened only after Jesus was already hanging on the cross.

The evangelist Luke imagines the arresting troop—analogous to the tradition of his second writing, the Acts of the Apostles—as troops of temple police led by "officers of the temple." In the event that the evangelist John, when speaking of "the soldiers" and "their captain," whom he distinguished from the "the Jewish police," had Roman soldiers in mind—given the terminology, this cannot be fully guaranteed—, then that may be linked to his changing of dates and the fact that Jews were not permitted to enter the Gentile-Roman praetorium on the day before Passover.

It is in any case, however, not historically credible that Roman soldiers took part in Jesus' arrest. The blow with the sword, which in the Garden of Gethsemane struck the ear of one of the servants of the chief priests, was not, according to the oldest account, carried out by a disciple of Jesus, but rather by an unfortunate soldier from within the arresting troop. Mk. 14:47 says: "But one of those who stood near drew his sword and struck the slave of the high priest, cutting off his ear." What is meant here is undoubtedly an unfortunate and accidental jab in the darkness of

night. The fact that there is no report of action taken against
Jesus' disciples excludes them as the sword-wielder. One
reports of their fleeing only after the speech of Jesus to
those who arrest him: "Have you come out with swords and
clubs to arrest me as though I were a bandit?"

The Trial Before the Sanhedrin

After his arrest, Jesus is led to the high priest—
Caiaphas, in whose house, according to the oldest account,
still during the night the Sanhedrin trial begins against him
as a seducer of the people. One cannot exclude the possibility that there was a short preliminary interrogation by the
father-in-law of the acting high priest, the powerful Annas;
however, in the fourth gospel, the Johannine scene replaces
the account of the Sanhedrin interrogation and reveals several signs of being a secondary conception added later.
When one reconstructs the trial of Jesus, it is better to ig-
nore this piece of Johannine tradition.

The legal case opened against Jesus is an exceptional case—the case against the seducer. This case could, according to the principle of *horaath sa'ah* ("because time
demands it"), be initiated during the night and concluded
on the same day. The serious case of the seducer of the people had to nullify normal legal regulations; for him, a kind
of emergency legislation was more or less appropriate. According to the early Jewish interpretations of Deut 13, the
seducer should be executed precisely on a pilgrims' feast
day in Jerusalem, in order to frighten the people. The emergency measures for the case of the *seducer* render then the
oldest account of the pre-Markan Passion narrative completely understandable and historically credible.

In case the Jewish leadership, as tradition says,
rightly feared a revolt by the people, those responsible had
to move as quickly as possible. Jesus had to be sentenced
and executed by the Romans, that is, had to be hanging on
the cross, before his followers awakened from the long
Passover night and learned about the actions taken against

him by the Jewish and Roman officials. The close proximity of the high priest's house to Herod's palace on Mount Zion undoubtedly enabled the Jewish leaders to make contact at daybreak with the court of procurator Pontius Pilate, which was in session anyway.

The trial against Jesus as seducer of the people begins with the interrogation of witnesses during the night of the sixth day of the week, the night of Friday, the 7th of April, 30 A.D., in the house of the high priest, in accordance with Jewish law. The hearing of witnesses, who during the night were ordered to appear before the court, undoubtedly intended to convict Jesus for his false and pretentious claim of being the Messiah, for being a *seducer*. Witnesses for the accused are probably therefore illegally-not heard, since they cannot be brought forth and probably also because Jesus himself could, by means of a clear denial, distance himself from any messianic claim.

Witnesses who cite a presumable saying of Jesus regarding the temple probably want to prove therewith Jesus' claim to being the Messiah: A new temple is built by the Messiah. The corresponding promise from 2 Sam 7 was interpreted during Jesus'day as messianic, and since 1958 we have learned about the actuality of this messianically interpreted scripture passage from data in a Florilegium (a collection of scripture passages) from Qumran.

In my opinion Otto Betz's (p. 633) interpretation is completely sound: "The high priest acts correctly when, in the face of no agreement, he considered the evidence presented legally invalid and did not yet dare to raise the question regarding the guilt and punishment of Jesus. Nevertheless he found a serious accusation against Jesus in the saying related to the temple and demanded that he himself respond to it; the direction in which his suspicion was aimed is evident in the following question." The high priest asks Jesus directly; thus far Jesus had responded with silence to the accusations of the witnesses, whose testimonies had not agreed and who thus had not given any legally valid evidence. The high priest proceeds from the questioning which had inaugurated the proceedings, to the interrogation of the accused: "Are you the Messiah, the Son of the Blessed One?"

With this Messiah question—which has now been proven possible, by a text from the caves of Qumran, as having come from the mouth of the high priest and which is protected from the long articulated suspicion of being a later Christian formulation—the high priest brings up for discussion the claim emerging from the temple saying of the witnesses, if one evaluates it in the light of 2 Sam 7:12-14 and that passage's messianic interpretation contemporary to the time. If Jesus in fact claimed that he wanted to "build" a new temple, then he must have in actuality understood himself as a Messiah of reform. Since the high priest had gotten no farther with the hearing of witnesses, he now questioned the accused himself. Could Jesus continue to evade the question through silence?

After he had remained silent in the face of the statements and reproaches of the witnesses—perhaps because he did not want to clarify "the tapestry of their statements woven of both truth and error" (Otto Betz, p. 633)—, Jesus now does not evade the question. According to the ancient account, he makes a clear confession: "I am!" He supports this confession in a non-political-theological interpretation with the claim that Jesus, as the Son of Man, will be enthroned at God's right hand and, by the authority of God, will be revealed as the judge of his judges: "and 'you will see the Son of Man seated at the right hand of the Power,' and 'coming with the clouds of heaven.'" It remains disputed whether this statement was made already during Jesus' trial or whether it belongs to the interpretive answer of the primitive church to Jesus' trial—that is, to the answer given in the continuing trial.

In any case, in order to grasp how the clash over Jesus' claim as Messiah was handled, one must know that early Judaism at the time of Jesus had neither a single expectation nor a clear concept of the Messiah: The expected "Anointed One" could have respectively more prophetic,

priestly, or kingly (and in this third sense, political) con-
tours. Jesus and the apostles did not measure his role according to a preexisting concept, but rather by his historically concrete commission which originated in the nearness
of God's reign which had come to pass; Jesus probably
made use of the apocalyptic Son of Man expectation because it allowed him to express his eschatological authority, to articulate the scandal of his purpose and his appearance. The "Son of Man" is the God-empowered representative of God's full power to judge; and Jesus interpreted
him as the servant of God through whom God definitively
marks the path of love for one's enemies, of suffering, and
of pro-existence in the history of God's people.

Regardless of how clearly Jesus, in his humility and
with his sense of reverence, may have distinguished between himself and the Son of Man on the clouds, in actuality, the claim of his words and deeds required the identifica-
tion of the two. For Jesus claimed—at least indirectly—that
the Israel of his time, which was called by him to change its
ways, encountered God's eschatological acts, God's undis-
guised will, in his own words and his deeds (and thereby
also in his own person); thus, he had said to his disciples,
probably in the context of persecution: ". . . everyone who
acknowledges me before others, the Son of Man also will
acknowledge before the angels of God; but whoever denies
me before others will be denied before the angels of God"
(Lk 12:8f.). Now the Sanhedrin was confronted with this
claim of his prophetic-messianic existence (which, of
course, could be traitorous if reinterpreted politically). To
perceive such a claim, to understand and to conform to it,
presupposes that one enters the selfless way of modesty and
humility of the messianic servant of God, of the Son of
Man, who "must suffer." Those who do not want to believe
it must twist it—in order to justify themselves.

This claim by Jesus is blasphemy for the Sanhedrin.
Otto Betz (p. 636) offers this interpretation: "Jesus slan-
dered God because, in spite of his powerlessness, he wanted to be on equal footing with God. Such a messianic claim

endangers, of course...the temple and the Holy City, [it] hands the people of God over to a Gentile power and is therefore blasphemous." The Sanhedrin believes that its view, namely, that Jesus is a seducer of the people, is confirmed.

Through the questioning of Jesus and through his answer, which was perhaps first formulated in the language adapted for liturgy, the members of the supreme council, of the court acting against Jesus, now themselves become witnesses. Jesus charged himself before their very eyes and ears. Their judgment, that Jesus deserves death, signals what is to come: Handing him over to the Roman procurator to be crucified because the blasphemous *seducer* should—according to the then contemporary interpretation of Deut 21:23—be hanged. Capital punishment lay, however, in the hands of the Romans; and their punishment for the political rebel was the terrifying crucifixion.

Inasmuch as during the night, as one may suppose, only a committee of the Sanhedrin (as was, of course, provided for in the law valid at the time) had carried out the interrogation of Jesus, under the leadership of the high priest, and had passed judgment on Jesus, early in the morning the entire council presumably came together to finalize the sentence. So it is told, in any case, in the oldest account.

The issuing of the sentence at daybreak served to open the trial against Jesus before Pontius Pilate. Before the court of the Roman prefect, Jesus of Nazareth was accused by the Sanhedrin of being a Messiah pretender, a "King of the Jews," a rebel of *seditio* (*stasis*), of revolt. According to the Roman *lex Julia de maiestate* (Digesta 48,4,1; 48,4,11), in the Roman Empire it was considered to be a capital crime against the imperial majesty when a subject of the emperor made a claim to kingship, if this claim gave rise to an armed or unarmed rebellion. The danger of a revolt had already been brought up by the Jewish leadership, when they attempted to trap the *seducer*. The high priest and the Sanhedrin could remind Pilate, of course, also of his function as defender of the temple, on which rested, always during the Passover feast days, the question of public law and order, as the Romans themselves clearly demonstrated with the fortification of their garrison and the close guarding of the temple grounds by guards atop the temple walls.

The Trial Before Pilate

In the meeting early in the morning, the Sanhedrin prepared—legally speaking—the *accusatio*, the written record with the accusation against Jesus, which also contained the *delatio nominis*, information pertaining to his person and activities. Early in the morning, as soon as Pilate sat in judgment in front of the praetorium, the chief priests would have presented him with the documents and handed Jesus over to him in chains. In the face of the confirmed danger of revolt, the governor was obliged to deal immediately with the presumed rebel, Jesus of Nazareth, if he did not want to neglect his duties.

In the rush, also Pilate had to appeal to emergency regulations. According to Roman law, he could interrogate the accused in a legal process *extra ordinem*. Unlike Jewish jural processes, witnesses were not heard first, rather the accused himself was interrogated immediately. Jesus was supposed to react to the accusations which the supreme council had brought against him in the court of Pilate. According to the exceedingly brief narrative of the oldest account, Jesus' answering of the governor's question, whether he was King of the Jews, by means of another question—"YOU say (so)?"—affirms at best indirectly his claim to being the Messiah; before the Roman provincial governor, he had much less chance than before the Jewish supreme council to interpret his claim theologically and protect himself from false political interpretation. To the accusations brought against him in the written records, Jesus did not answer when before Pilate, which surprised the Roman. Jesus *could*—if one accepted his question as an affirming answer, as if he had said "You said it!"—be consi ered a *confessus*, a confessed criminal; and Pilate could have proceeded according to the principle of the Roman law "confessus pro iudicato est" and allowed the judged to be executed due to his own confession.

But according to the presentation of our oldest source, the public court proceedings of the governor, which took place in front of his official residence early in the morning, was interrupted by a crowd of people who had come to make use of the privilege of Passover amnesty, to demand the release of Barabbas, the one they wanted pardoned.

Pilate was not, as the old account lets us know, convinced of the guilt of Jesus of Nazareth, who stood before him and refused to answer the accusations; this accused person presumably appeared to him to be no threat to public order, no rebel, since he himself had not revolted when arrested. And presumably there was nothing at all in the officers' reports of the last days before the Passover Feast about a Galilean called Jesus of Nazareth, for whom the Roman soldiers protecting the temple should be on the alert. Perhaps Pilate was, however, convinced of the guilt of Barabbas, who sat in the jail of his praetorium and had recently been arrested during a revolt.

The case of Barabbas is misunderstood most of the time because the evangelists opposed Barabbas to Jesus and led us to understand that, instead of the innocent Jesus, a ringleader and murderer was granted amnesty, or rather was freed through blackmail. However, the oldest account points our reconstruction of the event down another track. It says, namely, only that Barabbas was taken into custody with the rioters who had committed a murder during "the revolt." The account presupposes that this revolt had only recently taken place. This formulation leaves open the question of whether Barabbas, as an innocent bystander, was arrested and thrown into prison with the others when the Roman soldiers moved against the rioters. Even today it happens that, during demonstrations, people are arrested who are guilty neither of disturbing public order nor of breaking valid laws.

One circumstance indicates strongly that we should take into account the possibility that Barabbas was sitting in prison as an innocent, arrested passerby! It is the circumstance of the crowd of people going to Pilate's court on the morning of the Passover Feast day, in order to plead for Barabbas's pardon. Probably no Jew would have dared demand from Pilate the release of a notorious rioter and murderer, since whoever had done that would have risked being suspected as a sympathizer with terrorists and, perhaps, being thrown into prison. Pilate was not hyper-sensitive when it concerned using Draconian measures to maintain public order. That any people—and one should not imagine the crowd of people too large—dared to choose Barabbas as their candidate for amnesty and demand his release from Pilate, indicates that with Barabbas one is not concerned with a rebel and murderer, but rather with an innocent person who was arrested and thrown into prison with guilty people.

If we once again, with sharpened vision, reread the oldest account in this manner, it indicates this reconstruction: "Now at the festival he [Pilate] used to release a prisoner for them, anyone for whom they asked. Now a man nominated (= the choice of the crowd) Barabbas who was in prison with the rebels and who had committed murder during the insurrection" (Mk 15:6-7).

While the crowd wanted to plead for the release of Barabbas, Pilate appears to have held Barabbas more dangerous than Jesus; he wanted to keep Barabbas in prison and let Jesus go free. At this point the prefect made a mistake, probably because he sized up the situation completely incorrectly. The old account says: "So the crowd came (to the praetorium of Pilate) and began to ask Pilate to do for them according to his custom (to pardon Barabbas)" (Mk 15:8). Barabbas was then their candidate, and the custom of Passover amnesty intended that the governor release the person whose pardon was being sought. Pilate seems to have thought that he could grant amnesty to Jesus, who was also accused of being a rebel, instead of to Barabbas, who was more dangerous in his eyes. Thus says the ancient source: "Then he answered them, 'Do you want me to release for you the King of the Jews?'"(Mk 15:9). Suggested here as desired undertone is: Who is this Barabbas over and against Jesus, who is being accused before my court as "King of the Jews." Still, since the prefect offered amnesty, mockingly and ironically, to Jesus as "King of the Jews," he had fallen into his own trap, from which he does not escape without letting Jesus be crucified. In a public legal meeting Pilate had publically affirmed the accusation of the Jewish officials, that Jesus claims to be "King of the Jews" and is thereby guilty of high treason. Moreover, since Pilate offered amnesty to Jesus, he had insinuated that this prisoner was, or must be, sentenced legally; for only a guilty person receives amnesty—an innocent one would have to be set free in any case!

Since Pilate had thus—presumably without reflecting fully on the consequences—confirmed the accusation of the Jewish officials, he had to comply with the demands of the Jewish officials and the demands of the cheering crowd, unless he wanted to endanger, and place in jeopardy, his own position as defender of public order under imperial order.

Pilate had unsuccessfully tried to change the sentiments of the crowd, which had already come in order to attain the release of Barabbas by means of the Passover amnesty, so that it would request the release of Jesus. Naturally, the chief priests had little trouble in strengthening the crowd in their original intention and also to move them to demand Jesus' crucifixion. The old account says: "But the chief priests stirred up the crowd to have him release Barabbas for them instead. Pilate spoke to them again, 'Then what do you wish me to do with the man you call the King of the Jews?' They shouted back, 'Crucify him!'"(Mk 15:11-13). Since Pilate had taken over the accusation "King of the Jews" and offered amnesty to Jesus as one guilty of a crime, his retreat with the question, what evil Jesus had committed, was of no avail; as Messiah pretender, he deserved the death of the traitor, of the rebel, on the cross. Pilate had gotten himself caught in the logic of Roman penal law. He "had to" release Barabbas and send Jesus to the cross. The old account says this: "So Pilate, wishing to satisfy the crowd, released Barabbas for them; and after flogging Jesus, he handed him over to be crucified" (Mk 15:15). This means that Pilate had complied with the demand for amnesty of the crowd, whose candidate was and remained Barabbas; and he could not escape the logic, implied in his offer of amnesty, of Jesus' sentence as "King of the Jews," and he let Jesus be taken to the cross.

The flogging was the first act in the execution of the horrible Roman death penalty. The fact that on the way to the place of execution a passerby, Simon of Cyrene, was forced to carry the cross for Jesus, lets us know that, when flogging him, the soldiers had tortured him so severely that he no longer had the strength to drag the cross to Golgotha.

The trial of Jesus was quickly ended, after it was interrupted by the amnesty negotiations and diverted into illegal channels. Already by nine o'clock on the morning of the Day of the Passover Feast, on Friday, the 7th of April, 30 A.D., Jesus of Nazareth has been crucified.

PART TWO

THEOLOGICAL INSIGHTS

III

HOW SHALL WE EVALUATE
THE TRIAL OF JESUS?

How Shall We Evaluate the Trial of Jesus?

An evaluation of the trial of Jesus—in keeping with our reconstruction of its development in a twin case: before the Jewish Sanhedrin and before the court of the Roman governor—can be undertaken from two points of view.

The lawyer or legal historian may examine whether the processes were legal, whether there was no procedural error and whether the laws valid at the time were adhered to. The ethicist may reflect upon whether the valid laws which were employed were just or not; and already with such discussion the argument about the appropriate measure will begin.

The theologian will examine whether there is not, over and above the human and legal levels, something which requires a judgment of faith, the taking of a stand regarding prophetic-messianic authority with which Jesus claimed to act. The theologians are shown the way by the evangelists themselves and their evaluation is of faith. The lawyer is dependent on the hypothetical reconstruction of the factual development of the trial as the basis of his evaluation.

Inasmuch as the high priest and the Sanhedrin considered the emergency hearing legally valid for the seducer, one can most probably not accuse them of procedural error. Rather, everything points to the question, whether Jesus was really a heretic, a seducer of Israel, God's people? The law of Israel, as theological law and simultaneously (limited, of course, under Roman rule) civil law, appeared to have allowed the sentence which was unanimously agreed upon by the supreme council.

The Roman procurator Pontius Pilate appears, on the other hand, to have made a procedural mistake when he suggested giving Jesus amnesty before there had been a legal sentence pronounced on the accused; Pilate had therewith maneuvered himself into a trap. He probably did not consider Jesus guilty, but he nevertheless still allowed him then to be crucified as a rebel together with two rebels. The question of whether Jesus had really committed high treason would probably have been answered negatively by Pilate, and to this extent Jesus was nailed unjustly on the cross.

The Gentile governor Pontius Pilate did not have to reflect on the internal Jewish controversy of whether Jesus was a seducer of God's people; for him, the Jews were presumptuous, but no people of God. The Roman officials steadfastly refused—as one finds repeatedly confirmed in the Acts of the Apostles—to enter into the dispute related to the interpretation of the Torah, to make themselves the judge in internal Jewish affairs.

An evaluation of Jesus' trial leads then to a paradox: Jesus is—according to Roman law—not found guilty, but then, as an innocent person, is illegally executed. Jesus is—according to Jewish law—found guilty and in the eyes of Jewish officials (and many Jews who shared their view) is rightly executed. The Sanhedrin would surely have—if capital punishment had not been reserved for the Romans— carried out his death sentence itself, if it could have!

If we wanted—as has already been done enough in theological literature and novels and also on the stage—to legally open up the trial of Jesus once again, we would have to blame the Gentile governor more than the Jewish

officials. For Pontius Pilate, his position, which was dependent on the emperor, counted more than the life of a Jew,
who was nailed to the cross and whose execution, together
with two rebels, could serve to frighten the restless Jewish
nation which was rather rebellious against Rome.

The evangelists blame, however—and, in the course
of the development of a conflict between synagogue and
church, increasingly—the responsible Jews more for Jesus'
death than the Roman Gentiles. Why?

Evidently the Christian churches and their theologians are less concerned with the legal aspect of the case
against Jesus than with the trial's actual object of controversy, on which the Gentile governor could not, and did not
wish to reflect, the object which was rather at the heart of
the case before the highest Jewish officials, namely: Was
Jesus of Nazareth a seducer of Israel, of God's people?
Was he a heretic to whom the Torah's curse applied?

Or was Jesus of Nazareth the Messiah promised by
Moses and the prophets, the eschatological prophet sent by
God to gather Israel into a renewed, end-time People of
God: a people who should live completely according to
JHWH's social order and captivate all nations?

The evangelists evaluate the trial of Jesus against
the background of the earliest church's faith, according to
which the messianism of Jesus is confirmed by Jesus' resurrection and by the founding of the New Testament
church; they evaluate against the background of the scandal
of the crucified Messiah, who was rejected by the majority
of his own people (as was definitively proven after his
death in the history of primitive Christian missionary activities), who had been prepared for him by God over a long
history.

The trial of Jesus thus became, in the eyes of primitive Christian communities, a trial of God with God's people, with which they, of course, had become intertwined.
This intertwining must later be discussed. First, let us look
at the accounts of the four evangelists, at their perspectives,
and at the accents they have placed when evaluating the

trial of Jesus.

The Oldest Account in the Gospel of Mark

The oldest account is found in the Gospel of Mark; the evangelist received the old Passion narrative from the primitive church in Jerusalem. It is clearly recognizably influenced by the scandal of primitive Christian proclamation, namely, faith in the crucified Messiah. Moved by this paradox, the narrators try to show that Jesus of Nazareth was innocent and, with theological justification, deserves the title "Messiah," "Son of God," and "King of Israel." The account makes no explicit reference to the motives of Jesus' opponents, who brought him to the cross; only in one place, in Mk 15:10 it is noted that Pilate "realized that it was *out of envy* that the chief priests had handed him over."

"Envy" (*phthonos)* can be understood in the sense of "jealousy" (*zelos*), as holy zeal for Torah and temple, but also as deadly envy, which the biblical tradition had, since the narrative of Cain and Abel, made responsible for murderous violence in the world.

In addition to the introduction of envy as the motive of the opponents, the oldest account of Jesus' trial articulated, through an interpretation of events, the decisive theological-sacred-historical dimension surrounding the historical and legal dimensions of the trial, drawing thereby on biblical traditions related to the fate, the persecution, and the passion of the innocent righteous one. This is evident in the many allusions to the Psalms and the quotations from Psalms and the fourth servant song of the prophet Isaiah.

The experience of Israel which underlies the songs of lament and trust is this: Where the representatives of God and God's justice are found in our world—in the prophets, in the *anawim*, the poor who trust in God's law— there the evil powers, the opponents of God and God's righteous ones, make their appearance. Thus, for example, the persecuted righteous one prays in Psalm 69: "More in

number than the hairs of my head are those who hate me
without cause; many are those who would destroy me, my
enemies who accuse me falsely. . . . I have become a
stranger to my kindred, an alien to my mother's children. It
is zeal for your house that has consumed me. . .They gave
me poison for food, and for my thirst they gave me vinegar
to drink. . ." The persecuted righteous one prays in Ps 22:
"My God, my God, why have you forsaken me? Why are
you so far from helping me, from the words of my groan-
ing? . . . I am a worm, and not human; scorned by others,
and despised by the people. All who see me mock at me;
they make mouths at me, they shake their heads . . . For
dogs are all around me; a company of evildoers encircles
me. They pierce my hands and feet; I can count all my
bones. They stare and gloat over me; they divide my
clothes among themselves, and for my clothing they cast
lots."

The persecuted righteous one places his whole trust,
of course, in JHWH, his God, to save him. And the New
Testament church proclaimed the Messiah Jesus as the
saved savior, the resurrected redemptive leader.

In light of a theological reading of history, the trial
of Jesus appears as the universal conspiracy of God's enemies against God and God's anointed: Herod and Pilate,
Jews and Gentiles, as it says in an early prayer of the
church (in Acts 4:27) which is close to the pre-Markan passion narrative, "gathered together (in this city) against your
holy servant Jesus, whom you anointed."

In Mark's Gospel it is mentioned in an early passage that coalitions against Jesus are constituted; following
the healing of the man with the crippled hand on the Sabbath in the synagogue, it says: "The Pharisees went out and
immediately conspired with the Herodians against him,
how to destroy him" (Mk 3:6). The path for the alliance of
"church" (the pious Pharisees knowledgeable in the law)
and "state" (the followers of the Herodian royal house,
which likewise shines through in the cited prayer of the
church) is thus prepared.

From the midpoint (Mk 8:27) of his gospel, Mark
follows the thread of the pre-Markan Passion narrative, the
gospel of the primitive church. Now allusions are heaped
together: Jesus as the suffering righteous one and the servant of God who "must undergo great suffering" (Mk 8:31
with Ps 34:20), who is the object of the resistance of the
godless, their mockery, their scorn, their malicious tricks,
and their hatred, who is abandoned by his friends, who is
accused by false witnesses, and who, though innocent, is
put to death. Psalms 22, 27, 31, 34, 35, 36, 37, 38, 39, 40,
41, 42, 43, 54, 55, 69, 71, 86, 88, 109, and 118, and the servant songs of Isaiah (chaps. 50 and 53) give us key-words
and expressions, and therewith insights and perspectives
gained in Israel's history through suffering, for interpreting
the passion and trial of Jesus. If, for example, in Mk 14:46
it speaks of the "false witnesses" who speak out against Jesus, the opponents of Jesus are herewith characterized as
"evil-doers" who transgress against the Decalogue and typi-
fied as enemies of the suffering righteous one. Acccording
to Prov 6:17, "a lying tongue" and "hands that shed innocent blood" belong together. The motif of the lying tongue
(Ps 27: 12; 31:19; 35:11; 37:12; 109:2) and the enemies of
the pious, who lie (Ps 5:7; 58:4; 101:7), serves to interpret
the destiny of Jesus, who is victimized by the enmity of
people against God.

In the deep dimension of the narrative is found the
central theological question of whether God will, through
his righteous ones, through the single righteous one, who is
God's Messiah, come into God's own in this hostile world.
Has God come into God's own in the church through Jesus
of Nazareth and through his community?

The Later Accounts in the Gospels of
Matthew and Luke

The later gospels among the so-called synoptic Gospels, namely, Matthew and Luke, which are rooted in the
Markan account, placed respectively new accents in the

trial of Jesus. We shall here call special attention to only a few of the theological emphases.

Matthew emphasizes in relation to the arrest of Jesus that in the history of the Messiah the predictions of the prophets, which foretold the fate of the persecuted righteous one, God's servant, are fulfilled. Matthew lets one of the disciples of Jesus in the Garden of Gethsemane be the one who drew the sword, and then lets Jesus say: "'Put your sword back into its place; for all who take the sword will perish by the sword. Do you think that I cannot appeal to my Father, and he will at once send me more than twelve legions of angels? But how then would the scriptures be fulfilled, which say it must happen in this way?' . . . 'But all this has taken place, so that the scriptures of the prophets may be fulfilled'" (Mt 26:52-54,56). This "must" is the must of God's will.

Matthew indicates more clearly than his model in Mark's Gospel that Pilate was not convinced of Jesus' guilt. He allows the governor to wash his hands of the affair in public and say: "I am innocent of this man's blood; see to it yourselves" (Mt 27:24). And he lets all of the people who are present respond by saying: "His blood be on us and on our children!" (Mt 27:25) and, with this semi-legal expression, accept and share responsibility for Jesus' death.

Matthew also lets "the chief priests . . . along with the scribes and elders" mock Jesus on the cross with a literal quotation from one of the psalms of the suffering servant: "He trusts in God; let God deliver him now, if he wants to; for he said, 'I am God's Son'" (Mt 27:43 with Ps 22:9). Does God remain powerless in the face of the mockery which is poured out on God's "son?" How does God direct the trial for God's own purposes and for God's righteous ones? According to the account of Matthew, God does it through the messengers of him to whom God has given all power in heaven and on earth, namely, through the disciples of his resurrected Messiah (cf. Mt 28:16-20).

Luke knows that the trial of Jesus is finally also moved by the question which even came up among Jesus'

disciples in the room of the Lord's Supper, namely, "which
one of them was to be regarded as the greatest" (Lk 22:24).
Also he emphasizes more emphatically that, in the fate of
Jesus, the prophecy of the servant of God is fulfilled; he
lets Jesus say prior to his arrest: "For I tell you, this scripture must be fulfilled in me, 'And he was counted among
the lawless'" (Lk 22:37 with Isa 53:12). Luke shortens the
trial before the Sanhedrin; the supreme council announces
no death sentence, but rather brings Jesus immediately to
Pilate, where he is wrongly accused: "We found this man
perverting our nation, forbidding us to pay taxes to the emperor, and saying that he himself is the Messiah, a king"
(Lk 23 :2). The third evangelist clearly recognizes how—as
in the history of the churches, which are similarly accused
through public revolt—the history of Jesus repeats itself;
and he explains this correspondence (as one can more clearly see in the comparison of the account of the trial in the
gospels with the trial accounts in Acts) by intensifying the
political accusation against Jesus and simultaneously dem-
onstrating how empty it is: "Then Pilate said to the chief
priests and the crowds, 'I find no basis for an accusation
against this man.' But they were insistent and said, 'He stirs
up the people by teaching throughout all Judea, from Galilee where he began even to this place'"(Lk 23:4-5). Similarly, at a later time it will be said of Christians—of Paul
and his co-workers—that they are people "who have been
turning the world upside down" (Acts 17:6), who are "all
acting contrary to the decrees of the emperor, saying that
there is another king named Jesus" (Acts 17:7); about Paul
it is said: "We have, in fact, found this man a pestilent fel-
low, an agitator among all the Jews throughout the world,
and a ringleader of the sect of the Nazarenes" (Acts 24:5).

Luke—at least as strongly as Matthew—lets the Roman procurator, Pontius Pilate, speak of Jesus' innocence:
"Pilate then called together the chief priests, the leaders,
and the people, and said to them, 'You brought me this man
as one who was perverting the people; and here I have ex-
amined him in your presence and have not found this man

guilty of any of your charges against him. Neither has Herod, for he sent him back to us. Indeed, he has done nothing to deserve death'" (Lk 23:13-15). Similar to Matthew, Luke blames Jesus' death on the Jews, God's people, to whose arbitrary use of power Pilate finally surrenders Jesus.

By more or less relieving the Roman procurator of blame and giving more responsibility to the Jewish leadership and the Jewish people present in Jerusalem at the time of Jesus' condemnation, Matthew and Luke fostered the development of anti-Judaism in the later church, which was no longer sufficiently alert to the fact that it lived in continuity with the one people of God. The churches of the evangelists still knew that every believer is a saved sinner, that everyone shared the responsibility for the death of the Messiah, inasmuch as they had made room for hostility against God. And how should the evangelists have worked out or understood the trial of Jesus other than as the climax of a trial between God and God's people, which Jesus had already hinted at in his parable of the wicked tenants, where he refers to the song of the vineyard from Isa 5 which describes the trial between JHWH and Israel: "And now, inhabitants of Jerusalem and people of Judah, judge between me and my vineyard.... For the vineyard of the Lord of hosts is the house of Israel, and the people of Judah are his pleasant planting; he expected justice, but saw bloodshed; righteousness, but heard a cry" (Isa 5:3-7)? The evangelists had to point to the special responsibility of God's people—even for the sake of the Christian communities, the church, which should not exalt itself.

The evangelists—not moved by anti-Judaism, which is still completely alien to them—did not want to blame "the Jews," from whom they could have simply distanced themselves; rather, they know, as the author of the first letter of Peter said, that it is necessary for God's "judgment to begin with the household of God" (1 Pet 4:17). And therefore they themselves are implicated in the trial of Jesus, and, namely, in a double-sided manner: As members of the church they are tempted to crucify the Messiah anew in the "crucifixion" of his community and in the betrayal of the brothers and sisters in that community; as members of the community they are simultaneously affected by the persecution which affects all who commit themselves to the redemptive will of God in this world.

With this vision and out of the experience of the church in the first century, which taught that Jesus' destiny is also the destiny of his disciples, the evangelist John redefined the trial of Jesus in the fourth gospel: "If the world hates you, be aware that it hated me before it hated you. . . . Indeed, an hour is coming when those who kill you will think that by doing so they are offering worship to God" (John 15:18; 16:2).

The Trial of Jesus in the Fourth Gospel, the Gospel of John

The Johannine account of the trial of Jesus is indeed, with regard to the so-called historical facts, surely less reliable than the oldest account in Mark and, to some degree, also less reliable than the presentations of the two other synoptic gospels by Matthew and Luke, which are rooted in Mark's account. The Johannine account is, however, very exact when it comes to exposing humankind's hostility (from which, initially, no one can be excluded) against God and against God's son, Jesus Christ. Humankind? Yes, "the Jews," as is put forth in the fourth gospel when Jesus' enemies are spoken of, function here typologically as representatives of the cosmos, the world which has turned away from God and becomes hardened, where even among God's people God's plan is no longer promoted, but rather—as John does not hesitate to state—the things of the devil, the things of envy and violence. In this sense, "the Jews" are also the Christians, who further the purposes of God's adversary within God's people.

The fact that John presented "the Jews" typologically, as God's adversaries within God's people, was historically determined by the situation of his churches, which had come out of Israel and which found their greatest opponents and enemies in the synagogues. Such a typology was probably, even at that time, already dangerous, if it was not recognized for what it was and if its address to the Christian churches was not, with all humility, taken seriously. Today, we are no longer permitted to speak or write in such universal and undifferentiated terms!

John, however, wanted undoubtedly to show his churches, for example, how zeal against God, even behind a cloak—deceptively woven of self-deception—of zeal for God, blinds a person. Thus he says, for example, following the healing by Jesus of the man blind from birth: "The Jews did not believe that he had been blind and had received his sight. . .!" The parents of the blind man would not tell what had happened "because they"—Jews themselves!—"were afraid of the Jews; for the Jews had already agreed that anyone who confessed Jesus to be the Messiah would be put out of the synagugue" (John 9:18-22). John uses symbolic language within the context of his contemporary historical setting; "the Jews," as he names them, are the adversaries of Jesus and his community.

Also the Gospel of John is likewise far from expressing anti-Judaism; the evangelist rather exposes the *conditio humana*, the human condition, as it is made clear in Jesus' trial, in light of the sending of God's son into this world.

Following Auschwitz, it is clear, in any case, that—if it were historically possible—they could also be named "the Christians" rather than "the Jews"; and regarding the phrase which is utilized at another place in the New Testament: "who claimed they were Jews" could be linked to "who claimed they were Christians."

The Whole Life of Jesus as Trial

The fourth evangelist presents the whole life of Jesus, the entire public ministry of Jesus, as his trial, to which the proclamation of John the Baptist, including his hearing, is a procedural prelude (cf. John 1:19-28).

Following the preliminary history with John the Baptist and the story of the wedding at Cana, in the Fourth Gospel Jesus' public ministry begins immediately in Jerusalem: "The Passover of the Jews was near, and Jesus went up to Jerusalem" (John 2:13). Jesus' activities begin with the cleansing of the temple, a scene which is described more colorfully in John than in the first three gospels. Above all, however, immediately at the very beginning John points ahead to Jesus' death with Ps 69:9, a psalm of suffering (as we have already seen above): "Zeal for your house will consume me," the zeal for the temple which should be the renewed people of God itself, the zeal for the abode of God among human beings.

According to John 2:18-22, "the Jews" react sceptically to Jesus' cleansing of the temple and demand a sign; they demand a miracle which would verify Jesus' authority. Also Nicodemus, "a teacher of Israel," does not understand —as it is said a little later—that Jesus' authority can be grasped only by way of conversion, by way of new birth.

During Jesus' second stay in Jerusalem, open conflict results following his healing of a lame man on the Sabbath. "The Jews" persecute Jesus; they "were seeking all the more to kill him because he was not only breaking the sabbath, but was also calling God his own Father, thereby making himself equal to God" (John 5:18). Jesus had, responded to the rebuke that he had violated the Sabbath: "My Father is still working, and I also am working" (John 5:17). God's "work" is his redemptive, as well as his judgmental, activity; and this work Jesus also claims for himself. His appearance as God's representative, as the "son" of the invisible father, is salvation and judgment. Whoever does not want to let this truth reign as truth over her or his own life, although she or he has heard the claim, must banish Jesus from the world, so that one's own nothingness can maintain the appearance of substance.

Where it is said for the first time in John's Gospel that "the Jews" desire to kill Jesus, it is likewise clearly

noted that this intention is the inescapable and necessary result of "the world" which turns away from God's demands
and opposes God. The trial of Jesus has thus from the very
beginning an eschatological-universal dimension. The
question to be discussed in this trial is whether Jesus has
the exclusive right to call God his own father and to call
himself God's son, whether he really came as God's exegete (cf. John 1:18). John looks at history, so to speak, explicitly with the eyes of God, who guides the trial; and he
introduces the readers and hearers of his gospel to its deep-
er dimension.

　　Particularly remarkable is the fact that "the Jews"
criticize Jesus' violation of the Sabbath not only as a trans-
gression of the Torah, but rather, in the wake of his answer,
also the primary sin itself: He presumes to be equal to God.
Should this criticism not be applicable to Jesus? Is Jesus
equal to God? In the Fourth Gospel this question is dealt
with during his entire ministry as his trial.

　　John shows that Jesus does not flinch; he comes forward in public controversy and, in his speech of defense,
proves his right to speak of the Father, his right as the Son
who knows the will of the Father and who does the Father's
work. He uses the Torah to defend himself—and he names
Moses as the accuser of his opponents: "Do not think that I
will accuse you before the Father; your accuser is Moses
. . ." (John 5:45). Jesus' opponents are addressed as members of God's people, for whom Moses is the highest medi-
ating authority: "If you believed Moses, you would believe
me . . ." (John 5:46). "The Jews," who do not believe Moses, represent thus the non-believing "world." This world is
lost, however, to the degree that it threw away its chance to
believe and, as John will still show, does not even understand itself as unbelieving.

　　During Jesus' third stay in Jerusalem, the public,
trial-like conflict is carried further. Jesus says, among other
things: "Did not Moses give you the law? Yet none of you
keeps the law. Why are you looking for an opportunity to
kill me?" (7:19). The Torah, the law of Israel, forbids kill-

ing in the fifth commandment. Now "the Jews" want to kill
Jesus because he healed a person on the Sabbath—
performed a work of God! The crowd with whom he
clashed in Jerusalem demonize him: "You have a demon!"
(7:20). Soon the chief priests and Pharisees send "temple
police to arrest him" (7:32); but these emissaries become
witnesses for Jesus: "Never has anyone spoken like this!"
(7:46). The latter are cursed by their superiors for having
been deceived.

At this point Nicodemus, who himself was one of
the leaders who had come to Jesus by night (cf. John 3), in-
tervenes in the proceedings and demands a proper legal
process: "Our law does not judge people without first giving them a hearing to find out what they are doing, does
it?" But even Nicodemus receives a harsh rebuff: "Surely
you are not also from Galilee, are you?" (John 7:50-52),
whereas Galilee is probably named as the homeland for the
terrorism of zealots.

In a renewed public discussion in Jerusalem, finally
Jesus himself exposes the reason for the enmity of "the
Jews" against him; the evangelist lets Jesus speak expressly
"to the Jews who had believed in him" (John 8:31), that is,
to those persons who had familiarized themselves with his
claims and decided against him and wanted to kill him:
"You are from your father the devil, and you choose to do
your father's desires. He was a murderer from the beginning and does not stand in the truth, because there is no
truth in him. When he lies, he speaks according to his own
nature, for he is a liar and the father of lies" (John 8:44).
This speech presupposes the early Jewish interpretation of
the narrative of the Fall, in which the serpent in paradise
was identified with the devil, the adversary of God and the
confuser of men: The devil, who was driven by envy to be
like God, is driven by greed to murder—and he must hide
this fact in a lie in order to appear "good." Since Cain slew
Abel—because, as Genesis 4 says, burning envy overcame
him—, this has been considered the *conditio humana* of the
children of those who desired to be like God and who there-

by made themselves rivals who must fight the war of the gods in which each strives to supplant and eliminate the other. Jesus then tells them who want to kill him without logical reason precisely what the issue is: Because they themselves, as rivals, are supplanting Jesus; they themselves desire to be "Son of God" and want to accept neither the truth about themselves nor the truth about Jesus. They are entangled in the web of envy, murder, and lie. Correspondingly, at the close of the scene the evangelist says that Jesus narrowly escaped being stoned to death or lynched by the blind mob (John 8:59).

Then the tension of the incident grows. Jesus heals a man blind from birth—and indeed on the Sabbath. For this, he—who had done another work of God—is again demonized; the blind man, who holds to Jesus, is excluded from the synagogue. And many of "the Jews" finally say about Jesus: "He has a demon and is out of his mind." Others continue to take a stand for him in the public trial: "These are not the words of one who has a demon. Can a demon open the eyes of the blind?" (John 10:20f.).

Even before Lazarus is brought back to life in Bethany, there is a second attempt to stone him, on the occasion of the festival of the (temple) Dedication in Jerusalem, as a reaction to Jesus' saying "The Father and I are one" (10:30): "The Jews took up stones again to stone him. Jesus replied, 'I have shown you many good works from the Father. For which of these are you going to stone me?' The Jews answered, 'It is not for a good work that we are going to stone you, but for blasphemy, because you, though only a human being, are making yourself God'" (John 10:31-33). Once again the fundamental reproach against Jesus is that of primary sin, in the grips of which Jesus' opponents presently find themselves. Jesus now carries on the decisive public dispute with them regarding his claim to being the Son of God, which he justifies with the Torah, with God's Word. In the law itself JHWH says, "you are gods," thus marking those to whom the word of God comes. How can *the one* who listens to God, the *one* whom—as the Johannine Jesus says—"God has sanctified and sent into the world," not be called "Son of God"? The reaction is thus described: "Then they tried to arrest him again, but he escaped from their hands" (John 10:39).

After the raising of Lazarus, the Sanhedrin then decided—in spite of the objection of Nicodemus, who had demanded an interrogation and proof of guilt, that is, a legal process—"to put him to death" (11:53), without having interrogated Jesus and considering his case in his presence. Fearing that if they "let him go on like this, everyone will believe in him, and the Romans will come and destroy (literally: "take away") both our holy place and our nation," the high priest Caiaphas had advised that it would be better for one man to die for the people than for the whole nation to perish (11:48-50). The concern for the "holy place," the temple, and for the "nation," God's people, proves to be— as the evangelist sees it—self-centered, egoistic concern for one's own position. Lies cannot completely hide what motivates an envious person.

Soon thereafter the chief priests and the Pharisees give orders that anyone knowing Jesus' whereabouts should alert them, so that they can arrest him. This order is finally fulfilled by Judas. By his traitorous act, he made possible Jesus' arrest. After his arrest in the garden, on the other side of the Kidron valley, Jesus is led first to Annas, the father-in-law of the high priest Caiaphas. Annas questions him "about his disciples and about his teaching" (John 18:19), thereby suggesting that he takes him to be a *seducer of the people*. Jesus refers to the public dispute he carried on: "I have spoken openly to the world; I have always taught in synagogues and in the temple, where all the Jews come together. I have said nothing in secret. Why do you ask me? Ask those who heard what I said to them; they know what I said" (John 18:20f.). As had been demonstrated up to that time in public debate, Jesus has Moses and the law and—as his miraculous acts proved—God on his side. For his answer he was struck by a policeman of the high priest, and his protest remained unanswered. His opponents

continue illegally. Then Jesus is sent to high priest Caiaphas and from there to the headquarters of the procurator,
Pontius Pilate. In the Johannine account, a Sanhedrin inves-
tigation following Jesus' arrest is missing. John had already
anticipated the interrogation with that meeting of the supreme council after the raising of Lazarus, when Jesus was
condemned to death *in absentia*. The evangelist wants to
show how resistance to God's emissary drives one into the
illegal, blinding light of pure envy.

In the interrogation before Pilate, it is completely
clear that, appealing to God's call and God's law, the accusers of Jesus act against him illegally and godlessly, to
the point of a schizophrenic self-denial of their traditional
faith, to which they continue to pay lip service. Pilate asks
what their accusation is; they reply: "If this man were not a
criminal, we would not have handed him over to you"
(John 18:30). Pilate invited them to judge Jesus according
to their law, Jewish law; they respond: "We are not permitted to put anyone to death" (John 18 :31).

Herewith we have, on one hand, a reference to the
political situation, according to which the *ius gladii*, the
right to execute by the sword, capital punishment, has been
taken out of the hands of the Jewish leaders; on the other
hand, however, there is also a reference to the Torah,
which, in the fifth commandment, forbids killing.

The Roman procurator, who finds the accused
guilty of nothing, offers Jesus as a candidate for the Passover amnesty; "the Jews" request Barabbas, a bandit, a ter-
rorist (John 18:38-40). Pilate stresses again that he finds
"no case against" Jesus; the chief priests and their police
officials demand crucifixion (John 19:4-6).

Pilate finally gives in to them: "Take him yourselves and crucify him; I find no case against him" (John
19:6). Following this third declaration of innocence, "the
Jews" reply: "We have a law, and according to that law he
ought to die because he has claimed to be the Son of God"
(John 19:7).

What Jesus himself had, with the help of the Torah,

proved false in the public "trial" at the feast of Dedication is now brought up again by the Jews, who appeal to the Torah. The evangelist uncovers the central issue in Jesus' trial:

> Torah against Torah
> God's Will against God's Will—
> the sons of the devil against the Son of God!

They believe they are doing service to God—in blind zealotry which was brought forth by envy.

As Pilate, whom Jesus reminds of his responsibility, tries a final time to release the accused, pressure is put on him: ". . .but the Jews cried out, 'If you release this man, you are no *friend of the emperor.* Everyone who claims to be a king sets himself against the emperor'" (John 19:12).

Jesus, of course, had declared to Pilate that his kingdom is not of this world, but rather the kingdom of the witness to truth. For the Jews, in distinction to the Gentile Pilate, who had respected Jesus' reference to the authority granted him from above, the emperor became the supreme authority. As representatives of religion—no longer the liberated people of God—they have sold themselves into the slavery of the state.

By denying their confession of JHWH as the only king and ruler of the world, they ultimately force Pilate to give Jesus over to them to be crucified:

> *"We have no king but the emperor!"*

The fundamental Jewish-monotheistic confession states:

> *"We have only one king—JHWH!"*

Thus the Fourth Gospel makes the following evaluation:

In Jesus' trial, the blindness of unbelief wins out, the entanglement in envy, lies, and violence—as well as opportunism. Executed is the witness to truth, the non-violent doer of good, the revealer of love: the Son of God.

By means of the gospel narrative, the trial is once again brought before our eyes. Every reader can now once again form her or his own opinion, and do it concretely, regarding the community of Jesus' disciples, for whom Jesus prophesied the hatred "of the world": "If the world hates you, be aware that it hated me before it hated you. If you belonged to the world, the world would love you as its own. Because you do not belong to the world, but I have chosen you out of the world—therefore the world hates you....But: It was to fulfill the word that is written in their law, 'They hated me without a cause'" (John 15:18f.,25).

Different Versions "of the Trial of Jesus"

There are then different versions of Jesus' trial, on the one hand, the historical-critical reconstruction, such as ours, which we have based on the oldest source; on the other hand, the interpretation of the gospels, that of the youngest account being the most profound. The versions are not mutually exclusive, even if they appear to be contradictory. Just the opposite: The trial of Jesus always demands, as we have already felt, new interpretations; for the issue was and indeed is the claim of Jesus to be the Messiah, the King of Israel, the Son of God.

The accusation against Jesus is formulated differently in the various gospels; but at the center each time is the same claim: The "Messiah" is, according to Jewish tradition, "the Son of God" and "the King of Israel"! Undoubtedly, Jesus placed little value in these titles, but everything in having God's will as expressed in his words and deeds, that is, the reality of God, the grace and truth he represented (John 1:17), received as the reality of God himself, rather than rejected as a pretentious claim of Jesus.

Jesus was accused not only because he called into question the religio-political system of his day—the Jewish temple-state by the mercy of Rome; not only because he criticized the social compromise, the conformity, of God's people; not only because he placed Israel in question—as the enfant terrible of prophecy, of truth, as it were.

We cannot judge to what extent Jesus' opponents understood him, whether they noticed that they were being confronted with the question of faith, a theological question. That he offered and demanded faith was, of course, clear to his followers who initiated a revision of his trial.

Those who believe in him conduct his trial today, its revision, as it were, which God has already carried through. Those who believe in him have no other evidence than the witness of Jesus: the testimony of truth, of non-violent acts of mercy, of love; a testimony which does not seek honor among human beings, but only from the one God—according to the example of the witness of Jesus of Nazareth.

IV

"My people, what have I done to you?"

We had intended to tackle the question regarding what was at stake in Jesus's trial. And we had suggested that the Good Friday liturgy of the church is the main key to answering this question. In "the trial of Jesus" God became the accuser of his people! Christian liturgy, Christian theology, is familiar with a kind of guilt which applies to the people of God and humankind. It places Christians next to the Jews, the Gentiles next to the Jews, on the bench of the accused. It follows Paul who, in the letter to the Romans, exposed all human beings, both Gentiles and Jews, as sinners, appealing thereby to the judgment of the scripture of Israel: ". . . there is no one who does good" (Ps 14: 1).

That there are churches comprised of Gentiles, we can thank only God's mercy, the God who did not reject Israel, but rather called those among the nations willing to convert to join the remnant of Israelites ready to convert. Both Jews and Gentiles participate in the revision of Jesus' trial, and—according to the faith of the church—the revision is being done by God, who lets his Christ lament: "My people, what have I done to you?" Who today understands her- or himself to be addressed or accused by this lament? Has the liturgy become a mechanical activity or empty words? The people addressed by God is the one people of God, which, since the time of Abraham, has been chosen by God: "I planted you as a select vineyard, but you, how bitter you have become to me!" The community assembled on Good Friday prays to the Lord who accuses them; the community prays with the words of Ps 67:1: "May God be gracious to us and bless us and make his face to shine upon us." Us, here, today!

The presence of the liturgy, of the cult, is indeed the presence of the history of God with God's people. The concern is today, if you will hear God's voice. The glancing back into history, the gathering of history into the present, aims at this today. Already the gospels aim at such representation in the present, the most pronounced being John's Gospel, which we shall now follow once again after we have allowed ourselves to be led by a great thinker who has reflected on a key sentence from the trial of Jesus in the Fourth Gospel.

"We have no king but the emperor"

Blaise Pascal took up John 19:15 in his *Pensées* and used the opportunity to reflect further on the trial of Jesus. The fragment says: "Non habemus regem nisi Caesarem. Therefore, Jesus Christ was the Messiah, since they only had a stranger as king and wanted no other"; and then Pascal again cites: "We have no king but the emperor!"

How should we understand the logic of such reflections? Pascal first presupposes that the Messiah is the king of the Jews, the king of Israel. So it was also written on the cross of Jesus. The Jews had—according to their own statement before Pilate, with which they denied their own faith—no king other than the Roman emperor, that is, a stranger. And Pascal understands the passage from John's Gospel—and the unbelief of the speakers of the passage—to say that they also "want no other." However, how can one deduce from this: "Therefore, Jesus was the Messiah"?

Could a judge, should he once again be confronted with the trial of Jesus, make such a deduction, with good reason, from this passage? With what reason? Perhaps another passage of Pascal can help us answer this question: "Which person has ever caused a greater stir? The entire Jewish people predicts his coming before he arrived. The

Gentile world worships him following his coming. These two peoples, the Gentiles and the Jews, consider him their center.

But which human being has ever had so little advantage from so much admiration? Of his 33 years, he spends 30 in obscurity. For three years he is held to be a liar; the priests and the elders reject him; his friends and his closest relatives despise him. And, finally, he dies, betrayed by one of his own, denied by another; never has any human being been more humiliated. All of this attention was only for our sake, so that he would be recognizable to us; but he had nothing of it for himself."

Finally, a third passage points to the direction of the logic of thought: "By killing him, in order not to receive him as Messiah, the Jews gave him the final distinguishing mark of the Messiah."

Those who gave him the final distinguishing mark of the Messiah, the brand of the suffering servant, could not, however, recognize his messianic nature—or could recognize it only in retrospect, on the path of conversion. But all of this was "for our sake"! That means that we are called upon to evaluate, to recognize, to convert. We cannot escape the affair through an aloof, historical evaluation, still less by a condemnation of others, be they the "Jews" or the "Romans."

Already Paul, who himself turned from being a bloody persecutor of the "church of God," founded by the Messiah Jesus, to being a Christian and apostle of Jesus Christ, gained the insight that the wisdom of God had in fact revealed itself through the cross of Jesus the Messiah—scandal to the Jews and foolishness to the Greeks: "None of the rulers of this age understood this for if they had, they would not have crucified the Lord of glory" (1 Cor 2:8).

The evaluation: "Therefore, Jesus Christ was the Messiah" is an evaluation of faith which can only in retrospect be deduced from insight into the rebelliousness of us human beings, who from the very beginning, and again and again, have turned from and opposed the reign of God.

Jesus was the Messiah-King rejected by his people, the people of God; and in this rejection Israel—as once during Samuel's time—rejected God himself. The remnant of Israel called to faith—the eleven and the women of Easter morning and the hundred and twenty of Pentecost, the three thousand and five thousand of the following weeks, which are talked about in the Acts of the Apostles—bears witness, though, by its very existence to the fact that through the death of the Messiah, God has absolved his own people and reconciled them to himself (and, with them, the whole world) and offered them a new chance to turn to him. Believers are aware of a tremendous role change which must be recognized: Jesus—

> the accused one has become the judge,
> the damned one, the justified one,
> the powerless one, the mighty advocate and comforter,
> the silent one, the articulate witness.

Of what is the resurrected one speaking, after the "third day" and the "fiftieth day," through the mouths of his hundred and twenty, his three thousand, and his five thousand "members," through the mouth of his emissary Paul? He is saying that in his trial God was trying the unbelieving world; that God convicted his people of its disloyalty and its unbelief; that, on the cross, God "condemned sin"! He is saying that under the cross the "new family" of God was founded, the community of witnesses to the crucified Messiah, who established God's rule in the powerlessness of defenseless love, in the power of agape, the power of God's love for the enemy.

But was not also this speech, the speech—as faith says—of the "resurrected one," the word of a seducer and a heretic, the word of a traitor and a rebel? Does not the conflict with the Jewish religious officials and the conflict with the representatives of the Roman emperor immediately show itself anew? Stephen is stoned; James, the son of Zebedee, is decapitated; Paul is later executed by the sword in

Rome; Peter is crucified (according to the traditional legend, upside down because he considered himself unworthy of his master's way of dying). All of those who were baptized in his name and who gathered in his name were a part of the dynamite of the silent revolution which he had brought into the world.

Was he not in fact a *seducer*, not in reality a *rebel*? His defense was now taken over by those who were accused; he had said to them: "'Servants are not greater than their master.' If they persecuted me, they will persecute you" (John 15:20).

But why had they persecuted him; why are his servants persecuted?

What was at stake in his trial, and what is at stake?

We have already shown that the Gospel of John interpreted and presented the entire public ministry of Jesus in Israel as his "trial." If we orient ourselves by means of this account, we have (as far as the substance is concerned) a reliable thread leading toward an answer to the question of what was and is at stake in Jesus' trial.

We shall take up a few of the main sentences, a few of the major points, from the comprehensive account of the trial in John's Gospel, so that we may be clear about all of the things involved in God's trial against his people. In the account of the trial in his gospel, John utilized and evaluated an Old Testament literary form, namely, JHWH's legal dispute against his people. In the prophet Isaiah, JHWH challenges the citizens of Jerusalem to judge the vineyard Israel, which yielded sour berries rather than delicious grapes: "And now, inhabitants of Jerusalem and people of Judah, judge between me and my vineyard"; JHWH "expected justice, but saw bloodshed; righteousness, but heard a cry!" (Isa 5:3,7).

Already in the "prologue" John marks the analogous experience of JHWH with his own people by the sending of his Messiah, Jesus of Nazareth.

"He came to what was his own, and his own people did not accept him" (John 1:11)

Already in the prologue John hints at the heart of his gospel: World history and salvation history came to their climax and their ultimate historico-eschatological stage when God's Logos, incarnate in Jesus of Nazareth, appeared among God's own people, Israel, and when the Messiah was not received, but was rather rejected, by his people whom he had wanted to gather into an eschatological messianic existence and form of life.

John knows that, as long as humankind consciously exists, it will be driven by the religious quest for God and the fact that "no one has ever seen God" (John 1:18). In Jesus of Nazareth, however, the one appeared who, in his visible "flesh," allowed us to see the invisible God: "the only Son, who is close to the Father's heart, who has made him known" (John 1:18). Jesus says: "Whoever has seen me has seen the Father" (John 14:9).

Is this reliable truth? Did God's revelation then reach its culmination, its goal? Has God said everything he intended to say, through Jesus in the canonical words of his witnesses, regarding what he wanted to allow the world to experience of him in order to be saved? Or are such words the presumptious, blasphemous words of a seducer, a false teacher, and a heretic? Does Jesus not really belong on the gallows—or in a sanatorium for the mentally deranged?

Which judge could decide this case, apart from God himself? How should we, though, know God's decision—except through God's messenger, and since this one was silenced, through his messenger's messengers? "But to all who received him, who believed in his name, he gave power to become children of God" (John 1:12); they speak with authority of their Father and can testify to the only begotten Son. The decisive role in Jesus' trial was played by the people of God, the community of those "who believed in his name. . .who were born, not of blood or of the will of the flesh or of the will of man, but of God" (John 1:12f.).

Through Jesus' trial, not only is the question about God's truth decided, but also that about the reality of God's people. Belonging to God's people results from being born of God! Every wrong ethnic, racial, and national interpretation is rejected; every appeal to "flesh and blood," but also everything "spiritually" derived from the greater will of human beings, from their needs, is rejected. Since in the trial of Jesus the question is settled not only about God's truth but also about the reality of God's people, at stake is not only the religious quest of humankind (for the true god), but also its socio-political quest (for the redeemed society). Human beings attain happiness under God's reign, in freedom, as the people of God, whom God himself has created and ultimately shaped through his Messiah.

It is clear that the burden of proof for the justice of Jesus of Nazareth rests with the church, and all too often the church has—to the detriment of its mission and to the detriment of world history—transformed justice into injustice, most recently in its attempt to minimalize its share of guilt in the Holocaust. Of course, Jesus' justice cannot be proved quantitatively, through the deeds of the church, but rather only qualitatively, through its presence, its form of life, its suffering, and its "witness." And we today can bear witness anew—as on the first day, in spite of the burden of a long history—if we "believe in his name" and if we allow ourselves to experience: "From his fullness we have all received, grace upon grace" (John 1:16), and thereby come again into the state of knowing: "All things came into being through him, and without him not one thing came into being" (John 1:3), that is, if we grasp the unity of creation history and salvation history and make it known through the church's way of living.

When we recognize that we today participate in deciding Jesus' trial, then we cannot be indifferent to the church's mode of living. Is it recognizable as the verifying seal of Jesus' messianism, a place of Shalom, a room of peace and reconciliation, a congregation of unified believers, and a true community of sisters and brothers? Or has it conformed so much to the form and design of this world that it has lost its own shape and rendered itself superfluous?

Other central passages from the account of the trial in John's Gospel remind us of the different aspects of the burden of proof of the church, which itself is accused—by God: "What have I done to you . . ." Like a spotlight of a lighthouse, John always illuminates new points of accusation and thereby new questions regarding the mode of life desired by God for the church. Is it the messianic "body" of the Messiah?

"Stop making my Father's house a marketplace!" (John 2:16)

In the Gospel of John, Jesus' public ministry after the wedding in Cana begins in Jerusalem with the cleansing of the temple. And Jesus' first word is related to the "Father's house," the temple, but with this also, as is immediately clear, the people of God as the temple of God's presence. He is consumed with zeal for God's house (John 2:17 with Ps 69:9). The fact that the temple can degenerate into a marketplace, God's house into a place of trade, is for John an important point of controversy in Jesus' trial. The economic question cannot be kept separate from the question about God and the question about God's people. The problem inherent in the triad of religion, politics, and economy is not solved by their total separation from each other, but rather only by their "redemption."

The danger for religion lies thoroughly in the fact that its "salespersons" do business—then as now. One cannot escape this danger by declaring commerce, as well as the economic and political realms, "dirty business." This was not the significance of Jesus' action—which, according to John, was a violent action with "a whip of cords." Rather, Jesus insists that God's people as the abode of God's presence is built by God himself (as believers are born of God); and God's people are an independent society which is capable of common economic activity and thereby liberation and transformation in the economic realm, (specifically) by being enabled to work together freely and effectively. "Trading" in the temple is expressive of a "class society"—ruled over by an established priestly class which manages the temple as a "bank"—which gradually blinds God's people as his reflection in the world.

Israel was called as God's own people to build a new society of free persons, bound in solidarity, in the land granted them by God. The community of God's people lives, first of all, on the "credit" which each individual grants the other as a brother or sister (and therein God) given them by God; the foundation of trust (instead of envy, the fear of competition, and rivalry) enables the comrades of the new, liberated community to achieve a new way of dealing with economic realities. If every person is bound by God's reign and liberated to care for her or his neighbor (and allows her- or himself, again and again, to be liberated anew), the class society, which creates mistrust and rivalry, can be torn down and transformed—into the liberated, voluntary, new community of God's people. Jesus came in order to reestablish its magnificence.

According to the account of the synoptic gospels, through his action at the temple Jesus demonstrated for the assembling of Israel, which should once again become the fascination of the nations, in keeping with the promise: If Israel lives according to God's social order, the nations will recognize her wisdom and discernment—and God's nearness to this people (Deut 4:5-8).

In an idealized and spiritualized Christianity, one must today—as Karl Marx suggested for the "Germans" in his *Feuerbach*—"begin by confirming the first presupposition for all human existence, and, therefore, also for all histories, namely, the presupposition that human beings must be in a position to live if they are to be capable of 'making history.' Living consists above all in food, drink, housing, clothing, and a few other things. The first historical act is, therefore, the production of the means of satisfying these needs, the production of material life itself; and this is, to be sure, a historical act, a basic condition for all histories, which still today, as thousands of years ago, must be fulfilled daily and hourly, in order to simply keep human beings alive. Even if sensuality—as with the holy Bruno—is reduced to the core, to the bare minimum, the active production of this core is presupposed."

God's people, the church, the community, does not exist without this basic condition of all histories, but its existence can reflect the qualitative transformation of this basic condition—in accordance with Jesus' provocation: "But strive first for the kingdom of God and his righteousness, and all these things will be given to you as well"! (Matt 6:33). Jesus spoke of food, drink, and clothing!

At stake in Jesus' trial, is how Christians manage their daily lives, how they unlock the rich creative possibilities of this world for all, so that all can live!

If Jesus requires his disciples to seek first the kingdom of God, he then explains, of course, this seeking after "the first historical act," but certainly not as if the Christian could neglect or renounce it, as Karl Marx pictured it. Jesus' admonition in the Sermon on the Mount for a life free of cares speaks against a divided existence, which arises when life is dominated by idols. The reign of God and the everyday life of human beings no longer compete with each other among God's people. The Johannine Jesus had already made that clear in his "marketplace" speech with his reference to the words of the prophet Zechariah: "On that day there shall be inscribed on the bells of the horses, 'Holy to the Lord.' And the cooking pots in the house of the Lord shall be as holy as the bowls in front of the altar; and every cooking pot in Jerusalem and Judah shall be sacred to the Lord of hosts, so that all who sacrifice may come and use them to boil the flesh of the sacrifice. And there shall no longer be traders in the house of the Lord of hosts on that day" (Zech 14:20f.). Jesus wanted to realize that which had been promised for "that day"—the day of the coming of the Messiah—in the "Lord's house," in Israel, and among God's people; and it should be realized in God's church.

The trial is carried out against Jesus because he wanted to admit God into the everyday lives of God's people, radically, completely, and undivided—as the Torah had much earlier predicted.

His trial is decided when God is granted this admittance into the lives of God's people (where one no longer has to distinguish between "private" and "communal-ecclesiastical"), the people which "make history" with its quest for God's sovereignty, and in such a way that all can see how everything else is given them as well!

In Jesus' trial, the matter of the reliability of God's promises is settled—through the trust of God's children.

Is Jesus' call to abandon the cares of this world worthy of our trust or is it an illusion? Is he not really a seducer—even if only because he calls one to a hermit's existence? According to the account of John's Gospel, "the Jews" demanded a sign from him which would prove the authority with which he cleansed the temple. He promised to rebuild "this temple," the new creation of God's people, "in three days!" Is the New Testament community, the church, the "sign" of Jesus' authority? Or does it disavow him and cause him still today to be labeled as a seducer? Jesus had promised the Jews a "sign" which should verify his authority: the New Testament church which came into existence after his death. Has it remained for the Jews the "sign" which verified Jesus as the Messiah? And does it confirm to the Gentiles that their salvation has come into the world through the *Jew* Jesus of Nazareth?

"Salvation is from the Jews"
(John 4:22)

The words of the Johannine Jesus from the conversation with the Samaritan woman at Jacob's well are best suited to repudiate the reproach and accusation that John's Gospel and his account of Jesus' trial are anti-Jewish. Jesus is a Jew; he belongs to the Jews and comes from Israel; what is at stake in his trial is also the decision about the "true Israel." It is, however, a tremendous deception when one of our contemporary commentators maintains that a "qualified preference for Israel in salvation history" is "discounted from the very beginning" in John's Gospel; and that the "specialness of Israel" is "understood in such a way that it—to put it pointedly—rather hinders genuine faith." The Jew Jesus of Nazareth himself proves precisely the opposite!

According to the words of Jesus, Moses—and with him the whole Torah and the entire history of Israel—is his witness; and Christians need this witness in order to verify their own testimony for Jesus. Without the "Old Testament," whose concluding commentary is the New Testament, the New is like something amputated, like something "hanging in the air."

Jesus as "the Savior of the world" (John 4:42) is completely and properly understood only when one simultaneously recognizes and embraces the fact that "salvation is from the Jews." The separation of Judaism from the church is the church's greatest difficulty, greater than that of the church's internal divisions.

The fact that the Jews betray their own tradition in the trial against Jesus can for Christians—who themselves remain constantly in such danger and who repeatedly, and most recently in a horrible way, have succumbed to this danger—only be the stimulus to win Israel's tradition along with the Jews and for the Jews. Today Jesus' trial is decided by the response of contemporary Christians to the Holocaust, the Shoah.

To reappropriate the tradition of Israel means to reappropriate the undivided life of God's people with and before God, as well as the this-worldliness of this life—its world-affirming nature, its adventure, its intensity, and its quality.

The tradition of Israel is its differentiated knowledge gleaned during a long process centering on the distinction between revelation and the religions, through criticism of the gods and the idols, of the state and the temple servants, of the corruption of the human heart and of "pet gods." The tradition of Israel is its wisdom, which has always reflected anew on its experience of the world before God and in light of its people's history; it is its art of education, its prophetic courage, its willingness and strength to suffer, its messianic fire.

What we mean, among other things, can perhaps be expressed in the following Rabbinic narrative: "When Rabbi Bar was five years old, a fire broke out in his father's house. When he then heard his mother complaining, he asked her, 'Mother, do we have to grieve so because we are losing a house?' 'I am not lamenting over the house,' she said, 'but rather over our genealogy, which has burned. It began with Rabbi Jochanan, the sandalmaker, the master of the Talmud.' 'Well, what of it!' cried the boy, 'I want to create a new genealogy for you which begins with me!'"

The church, we Christians, could and must recognize today, at the latest, that we must win Israel, the Jews, for the sake of world redemption, for the birthing of the redemption brought to the world by their and our Messiah. According to the Gospel of John, the Messiah, the Jesus raised high on the cross, wanted "to draw all people to himself" (John 12:32), that is, to gather all into the international people of God.

Christians owe Jews, more than ever before, evidence of the fact that Jesus is the Messiah and that he founded the messianic people as an instrument of salvation—the fathers called the church, for example, "Arch."

The dependence of the world on the Jews, the one people of God drawn together by Jesus, is palpable—in the face of this "wisdom and discernment" (Deut 4:6) of Israel, which has been conserved to this day and which has been increased through suffering and learning, learning and suffering. Should not, must not, the gathering begin anew today of all of those whose deeply felt calling is the redemption of the world for the honor of God? Begin in a practical way? Not in theoretical controversies!

One of the most puzzling hindrances to the gathering together of God's people is created by contemporary Christian theologians when they—by ignoring the fact that the earliest churches were made up completely of Jews—maintain that the Jews of Jesus' day could not have recognized him as Messiah or that it is impossible for Jews to believe in the incarnation of the Logos. Thus, for example, one could read in a widely circulated periodical in October of 1987: "Christians are distinguished from Jews through Jesus Christ, in whom, according to Christian belief, God became man. It is impossible for Jews to accept this. For them, the one and only God is invisible, only being depicted by human images or with earthly characteristics"—as if for Christians God is not just as "invisible" and as if Israel had not also depicted God anthropomorphically in the wonderful linguistic imagery of its Bible! It would be possible for Christian theologians to make a greater effort to formulate their faith in a less misunderstandable and more enlightened manner. And the tradition of Jewish Enlightenment could be very helpful in this regard.

"My father is still working, and I also am working" (John 5:17)

The Johannine Jesus follows Jewish tradition when he speaks of God being at work. God works on the perfection of the world which he created. It is true that on the seventh day God rested from his creative work on the world, but not from his work on human beings, on the evil-doers, whom he must punish or forgive, as the case may be, and the righteous, whom he rewards.

At issue in Jesus' trial is the question of how God's people become participants in God's work through the Messiah, that is, how God's people become co-laborers with God. Do they hinder God, for example, by preventing healings on the Sabbath? Do they hinder God—as they did later in the church—by denying that God's rule aims, even now, to intervene in social conditions, in the voluntary, common work of the members of God's people, changing them and transforming them?

Do the liberated co-laborers share the unbelievable freedom of their master—thus, as Jesus did? Do they recognize the connection between forgiveness of sin and wholeness and new life? Do they, as Jesus the Son, do nothing in and of themselves (cf. John 5:19), nothing by their own power, but rather according to the order of the Father's work, which, of course, is the creative order of the new creation?

It is hardly by chance that John's Gospel focused the first time on Jesus' public trial after Jesus' words regarding the work of the Father and his own co-labor with the Father: "For this reason the Jews were seeking all the more to kill him, because he was not only breaking the sabbath, but was also calling God his own Father, thereby making himself equal to God" (John 5:18). Jesus does not bring salvation magically, but rather by contributing to the Father's work.

We need to ask how this common work must appear today. That this question is already satisfactorily answered, no one can claim. That the church accomplishes God's work, hardly anyone would dare to declare—unless it were a mystifying theologian handling the sacraments. Jesus had, however, healed on the Sabbath, had really worked and allowed to work. He allowed the lame to walk and the blind to see, literally *and* figuratively. He presupposed that God labors for his people and does not want to have a people comprised of the poor, the sick, the crippled, the depraved, but rather a people which satisfies everyone and whose demeanor is attractive, not repulsive.

For a long time, God's purposes have undergone redefinition—chiefly in a false theology of the cross: as if God's option for the poor was poverty, as if God's option for the suffering was suffering, as if God's option for the crucified one was the cross!

In Jesus' trial, the decision about God's work, about the actual transformation of the world, is at issue. Jesus had taught that we could recognize God's co-laborers—and, correspondingly, the co-laborers of the devil—by their fruits! By the fruits produced in the grace of liberation!

This teaching was valid also for him. The church is his "work," the "result" of his work as *the* co-laborer of God. Is it the fruit *today* which proves that he is the Messiah? The *history* of the church is not the only thing that counts, but also *today*.

It is said that Rabbi Baruch stated: "The great accomplishment of Elijah was not that he performed miracles, but rather that, when fire fell from heaven, the people did not speak of miracles, but rather all cried, "The Lord is God!"

The trial of Jesus elicits also the question of recognition and the measure of evaluation with respect to "God's work." Much too quickly today every kind of uncalled-for condemnation is passed on the history of the church—and also many theologians appear no longer able to recognize the church as God's work. Is it so disfigured? Are our eyes so blind? Or do we not want to see—like those, long ago, who demonized Jesus?

One of the worst and most effective (in the negative sense) misunderstandings of the Christian faith is a magical understanding of redemption: as if our labors with God were no longer needed. God and the Messiah, Jesus, are, however, dependent on our participation in their work: They would have needed us in order to save the Jews from the gas chambers; they would need our unified cooperative labors in order to save many from starvation today. Whoever magically spiritualizes redemption is guilty of sinning not only against human beings, but she or he also speaks blasphemy and tarnishes God's glory. God staked his glory—through his Messiah, the human being, the Jew Jesus—on winning us as his co-laborers. As his co-laborers—as Jesus knew—he involved us in his eternal life.

"Whoever believes has eternal life"
(John 6:47)

Did not the serpent in paradise promise Eve "eternal life"? Is not such assurance the promise of the seducer? The crux of Jesus' words is that "eternal life" is not promised for the future, for life after death (as is the case for many religions), but is rather promised believers now: Whoever believes has it!

Why is the simple condition "whoever believes" so difficult for most people? Why does one so seldom trust this promise, although everyone wants eternal life, wants immortality (or, again today, rebirth)? The simple condition is so difficult because it demands trust in the visible witnesses of the invisible God.

"Eternal life" did not bind Jesus, along with his Jewish ancestors, to the immortality of the soul—he knew nothing of this—, but rather to God's faithfulness. "Whoever believes" means for him whoever trusts in God, in God's power and faithfulness. And, indeed, concretely: Whoever trusts in the visible messengers of the invisible God, now and here!

"Eternal life" is already present in the church, in the Christian community, in the circle of brothers and sisters: "We know that we have passed from death to life because we love one another"(1 John 3:14; cf. John 5:24). The defining of life and death is not the task of the natural sciences, not the task of worldviews and religions, but rather the task of the theology of revelation and the praxis of faith which it has inspired.

In the tradition of Israel, Jesus learned to serve God *without reward*—though he was completely convinced of the Father's faithfulness: God is a God of the living.

One dimension of Jesus' trial is the reality and dynamic of God's presence, the presence of God's eternity, verified and rendered perceivable by Jesus. Do God's people today believe that God gives them the free gift of eternal life? Or do they rather put their hope in heaven, so that

God does not, now, come too close to them? The hidden mainspring of worry of many so-called pious people, with regard to an orthodox faith in and "secure" hope in the resurrection, is—according to Jesus' insight—ignorance of God, who already wants to encounter us fully. God does not love us partially! God tries to encounter us here and now—not later, in another world. For our sakes, God has indeed made his other-worldliness this-worldly. Jesus had proclaimed God's nearness; the son had brought the Father near. It would be a great misunderstanding to think that through death and resurrection Jesus became "other-worldly." He is indeed the Lord at the center of our congregation who triumphed over death and made it possible for us, in *agape*, to cross over from the "other-worldliness" of death into the "this-worldliness" of the eternal life opened up by him.

The opponents of Jesus were, by the way, both the Pharisees, who believed in the resurrection of the dead, and the Sadducees, who rejected such belief as not being rooted in the Torah and who were pictured by later Rabbinic tradition as this-worldly atheists. Both groups felt and knew themselves to be threatened by Jesus' theology and by his praxis of the nearness of God's reign, his "praxis of heaven," which transcended all theories.

And yet, Jesus only advocated what the prophet Isaiah had advocated already in the name of JHWH: If you do not believe, you shall not endure! If you do not root yourself in JHWH, you will have no foundation! If you do not secure yourselves by trusting in God, you shall sink into the bottomless pit (cf. Isa 7:9). Jesus had learned from the history of his people because he had opened his heart completely to the words of the Father written therein. Whoever wanted to cling to the past could take offence at Jesus' courage to change and create something new; and whoever wanted to create, inaugurate, or bring forth, something new could be confused by Jesus' rootedness in tradition.

The trial of Jesus became a trial against unbelief

and the exposure of mistrust, of little faith, of opportunism and conformity. This trial is brought up and carried forward again by Jesus' witnesses. It is decided in martyrdom, the evidence of God's faithfulness.

One of the special dangers of contemporary theology consists in no longer viewing martyrdom with God's eyes and judging it in the name of God. Increasingly, the fashionable talk of—from the human perspective—"Jesus' failure" spreads! How else can one then judge the church, than to say that, after two thousand years, it has failed? And do not many theologians—secretly—fear this? And do they not herewith—taken in by appearances—give up Jesus' trial as lost?

"Do not judge by appearances, but judge with right judgment" (John 7:24)

In the public trial of Jesus in John's Gospel, Jesus is demonized following a Sabbath healing in Jerusalem: "You have a demon!" (John 7:20). Jesus asks why one is angry with him for healing a person on the Sabbath. And then he admonishes the people, his opponents, not to judge by appearances! His trial was judged according to appearances, and it must be revised by and in a just court of law.

How can a necessary revision of appearances take place?

The revision of Jesus' trial, as we have already repeatedly noted, is not the task for historians or legal experts, but rather the task of the church, the people of God and its theology—a theology, of course, which is oriented toward a just judgment and which is in a position to carry through its task of putting things right.

An analogy may help us see what the issue is. Our eye projects everything on to the retina "on its head," that is, as a mirror reflection. Our brain, our thinking apparatus, performs the task of putting things right; it puts things right side up, places them properly upright.

As a rule, our entire perception of the world is correspondingly unclear and perverted. It needs to be put right. Our idols, our wrong models, our false gods, and our demons live in our hearts and muddy our "eyes."

Jesus' opponents in the trial, for example, could—according to the extent their perceptive ability was muddied—not believe it possible that Jesus of Nazareth, this son of an artisan from the hills of Galilee, this uneducated layman, was in fact the Messiah, and not a seducer; that he was in fact "the King of the Jews," and not a rebel or a crazy person. Why not? Because they measured things according to their own standards—and not according to him! They remained slaves, as the Johannine Jesus put it, to their own reputations, which skewed a free judgment. On the other hand, Jesus measured things by God's glory, by God's history with Israel and by the nearness of God's reign.

And those in Jesus' trial who judged by appearances were not just some insignificant people; they were rather the representatives and leaders of Israel, God's people, of that day. Who protects, however, the contemporary representatives and leaders of the church from appearances and from unjust judgments?

The calamity of "appearances" consists in the fact that muddied vision is unable to perceive the perversion of judgment—and that prestige-hungry persons do not want to admit the false and inverted state of their judgment.

It remains to question, to what extent the theological enterprise, which expresses itself in a flood of books and educational activities, is representative for our whole society; it is striking, in any case, how quickly everybody voices his or her judgment, with its prejudices and its evaluation and its condemnation. Exegetes apply "objective criticism" to the Old and New Testaments, instead of always being prepared to learn from the tradition of God's people. Thus, it has come to a mishmash of opinions, which, on top of being a mishmash, is then made interest-

ing and is justified as theological "pluralism." A just judgment does not seem to exist anymore.

   The just judgment is possible only to the one who
has been granted the ability to see with God's eyes. Believers trust Jesus, the one who was close to the Father's heart
(John 1:18), to do this. Jesus trusts those who are his faith-
ful followers, those who gather in his name, to do this; he
trusts the organism of his "body" (which has "eyes" that are
not simply identical with the eyes of an individual, but are
rather a communal organ). Believers know about the "infal-
libility" of the church, since it was granted the *contuitio*,
the *contuitus*, the ability to see with God's eyes.

   A revision of Jesus' trial can take place only when
many take part in this seeing-with-God's-eyes; the New
Testament churches engaged Jews *and Gentiles* in this process—and we? We are commissioned to engage Gentiles
and Jews, and, additionally, those who have distanced
themselves from Christianity, as well as those who no longer count themselves a part of religious Judaism. The revision, of course, does not begin if we do not allow our blindness to be taken away and our eyes to be opened anew.
With the willingness to do this or not the roads part.

"There was a division in the crowd because of him" (John 7:43; 8:16)

   With Jesus of Nazareth the roads part, also with his
community, the church, the roads part as they did with him.
Otherwise, his trial has been quashed!

   The special thing about the division which took
place because of Jesus of Nazareth was, of course, that it
was a division within God's people, in fact—as demonstrated during the years after his death in the history of his community—it was a division *of* God's people. In the trial
against him, representatives of his people stood against
him; because he was condemned as a seducer, as a heretic
and pseudo-messiah, the Messiah was expelled from his

people, the people who had been called by him to messianic perfection.

After his death, he, the resurrected one, gathered by means of his spirit those of the messianic people who recognized that they had been absolved through his death and liberated from enmity with God and each other. Thus was born—as the institution of his life and death—the messianic *ekklesia*, with him as *Lord* at its center and with his *Shalom* as the basis of its existence and its authority to forgive sins, the authority which empowered it to invite everyone into the end-time, restored people of God, into the "true Israel."

The largest part of Israel, from which the Messiah, Jesus, was expelled, remained behind as the non-messianic synagogue, separated and in a state of anti-messianic resistance, or even simply ignorant and untouched. The non-messianic synagogue became to a certain extent, at the beginning, a persecutor of her messianic sister, the *ekklesia*; when the church later allied itself with the Roman state, it backslid in a terrible manner away from the love for the enemy advocated by its Lord, discrediting itself and thereby its Lord, on whom it called.

The division within the messianic people of God, the schisms within the church, that is, ecclesiastical divisions, are indeed less fundamental (and would therefore be easier to heal), but in no way less devastating historically. They rob the church of an important messianic trait, namely, its unity; and they thus prevent the church from overcoming the fundamental schism.

If ecumenical dialogue could venture such insight, what would then prevent unity? The amount of effort necessary was already mentioned by Paul in his Letter to the Romans: "For I could wish that I myself were accursed and cut off from Christ for the sake of my own people, my kindred according to the flesh" (Rom 9:3).

Of course, the schism within God's people cannot, as the history of the foundation of the *ekklesia* demonstrates, be overcome through commission papers and conferences, through consensus documents or "convergence," through compromises or something similar; it needs a radical, God-given, new beginning—and the recognition of this scandal (that, to my consternation, came into the world without my help).

Jesus blessed those who took no offence at him, but could rather recognize, without envy, that *he* knew the way for his followers to gather Israel. God's acting in history—also today—can be irritating because it frustrates my plans for my life, my ideas, my academic theories, or my career. It can be so irritating because it questions me about my faith and suspends my everyday and commonplace criteria. Divisions persist because unbelief persists; faith in the one God, in the Lord Jesus Christ, and in the one Spirit cannot be divided because God does not give cause to divide. We must seek the cause for division among ourselves. Jesus encouraged us to do this with sharp words.

"You are from your father the devil" (John 8:44)

Jesus reserves his sharpest criticism for "the Jews who had believed in him"(John 8:31), that is, for those of his followers who became his enemies, of whom it then says: "So they picked up stones to throw at him" (John 8:59).

Is the trial of Jesus therefore also nothing more than an alternating demonization of the parties of the trial? Did not he who reproached the sons of Abraham as children of the devil in fact expose himself as a seducer?

The eighth chapter of the Gospel of John is looked upon as the clearest expression of his anti-Judaism. However, this understanding of him is a crass misunderstanding of the evangelist's theology

In the Johannine perspective, the trial of Jesus is an exposure and conviction of the world and an exposure and conviction of the resistant hard-headedness of those who have deserted their call among the people of God. As we have already noted, Jesus speaks to "the Jews, who had believed him." By believing him, they had put their trust in God's goodness and in Jesus as its representative. What reason had he given them to distrust this goodness, to mistrust him? Jesus himself said: "But now you are trying to kill me, a man who has told you the truth that I heard from God" (John 8:40).

In the trial of Jesus, it is made clear that human beings do not want to hear the liberating truth about themselves. And in John 8, this truth—that this is our situation—is dramatically formulated, so that also the stubborn non-hearers are given a chance to convert, if they can recognize themselves in this mirror as "sons of the devil" and "brothers of Cain." "And the truth will make you free" (John 8:32). Untruth, falsehood, makes the world hell, a hell in which lies and murders are at home.

Jesus' words about father devil apply just as much to the Christians who had believed in him and renounced their calling as they do to the Jews. Not without reason does the Judeo-Christian tradition speak of the devil as of a fallen "angel," a chosen messenger who betrayed his calling. Calling is, according to this tradition, the calling to service; and apostasy is the refusal to serve. In the trial of Jesus, it is decided who will serve the purposes of world redemption and thereby the will and plan of God—and who will serve his or her own will and ambition.

Jesus came as Messiah, in order to remind God's people of their messianic service, the ministry of God's servant. The reprimanding of the Jews by the Johannine Jesus serves as such a reminder—as it serves as a reminder to the Christians who hear the gospel in their assemblies. It does not, in and of itself, inaugurate anti-Judaism.

The church which becomes addicted to or remains the victim of anti-Judaism, decides Jesus' trial (to the extent that it can decide it) against Jesus. It expels the *Jew Jesus* from the church—as Israel expelled its messiah from God's people.

History has made it clear that the deepest root of anti-Judaism, is the resistance to the presence in our world of the one, true God, who calls our self-deification into question. The hate which was and is aimed at Israel is no normal hatred of the stranger, but rather the revolt against a degree of right, justice, and community devotion not created by us; the refusal to commit our wills unreservedly to the Creator and Lord; the blocking out of the enlightenment of the world, in which each person appears as he or she is.

Christian anti-Judaism is a peculiar perversion. It blames the Jew for giving the Messiah, Jesus, to the world. Was it by accident that, during the so-called "Third Empire" of Nazi Germany, Christian theologians tried to prove that Jesus was an Aryan and not a Jew?

Christian anti-Judaism is the most profound apostasy of Christianity. by itself deceitfully minimized and misrepresented. It supersedes all heretic and witch hunts. How can a tree desire to pull out the roots which give it life? It is not possible to give a rational answer to such a phenomenon—it is causeless! Israel's theologians discovered this, of course, long ago when, in Ps 35:19 and Ps 69:4, they spoke of a hate "without cause" against the righteous ones among God's people.

"It is better for you to have one man die for the people than to have the whole nation destroyed" (John 11:50)

The saying of the high priest, Caiaphas, which was considered in John's Gospel as unintended prophecy, exposes the political logic of Jerusalem's religious leadership at that time—and, in addition to that, according to the perspective of the evangelist and his community, the logic of the world caught between religion and politics.

Whether Caiaphas's main concern was the people, the whole nation, or even the people of God, or whether it was, first of all, his own family and the class of high priests and their clientele, may be and remain controversial among historians. Meticulous Jewish researchers tend to blame the priestly aristocracy—who, following the Jewish war and the destruction of the temple, abdicated *en bloc* in favor of the lay movement of the Pharisees—in order to exonerate the Jews, the entire people. Also here there appears to be the scapegoat mechanism at work, which the evangelist had tried to expose but which was also rampant in the church in a thousand different ways.

The evangelist emphasizes that Jesus really died for his people, Israel, in order to gather them, as well as also all of those from among all nations who were willing to convert, around the original will of God, made definitively known by him in a new way.

John's Gospel, along with the entire New Testament, lets us know that the trial of Jesus was and is decided by God's love for his enemies, a God who did not cast his people away, but rather accepted and strengthened them anew by including the Gentiles. The church comprised of Jews and Gentiles—the reconciled community of those who had previously been bitter enemies—is a mirror of God's love for his enemies. The shattering of this mirror shatters our world, destroys it by wars . . . The world suffers under the scapegoat mechanism, which teaches that one should be sacrificed for the whole—or one people for another. Can our world survive with the impulsive notion that one is the "wolf" of the other? The apparent stability of the unstable balance is repeatedly brought about when single-minded ruthlessness finds its sacrificial victims.

The Christian faith maintains that Jesus was truly the one and only necessary sacrifice for all persons, that he truly died *for all*. To the extent that we believe that this was God's act, that God "offered him up," this effectively becomes a healing and pacifying sacrifice.

The death of the Messiah Jesus by crucifixion is, according to the Christian faith, the one and only sacrifice, which is sufficient to bring into life a harmonious society as the stabilizer of the world, the free community of the mutually reconciled.

Considering this, one could say that Jesus' trial takes place in a world history which has been adjusted by salvation history. Its re-direction is effected by the renewed people of God, who had just been brought into the world through the death of Jesus. The traditional Passion narrative, which relates his trial, is written out of this knowledge. The primitive church articulated its own experience, namely, that previous enemies and opponents can, by trusting God's acts and being reconciled through Jesus, live with each other. However, it also reports that such provocation is invariably faced with ever new envious resistance, and it included this in its narrative of the story of Jesus. The later communities likewise allowed their rich historical experiences to flow into the gospels.

That in the Pauline churches every person was considered as the sister or brother *for whom* the Messiah died, was the basis for a world revolution. That Jews and Gentiles, who—as it says in Ephesians—were separated from each other by a world-dividing wall, by an "iron curtain," became now nevertheless a community with a shared life, including table fellowship, made peace in this world truly and effectively possible. The quarrelsome world received thereby a new, stabilizing factor, a light of peace.

"We have no king but the emperor" (John 19:15)

According to evidence in the Acts of the Apostles, the apostle Paul (as the representative of the Christian churches) was reproached for saying that there was another king apart from the emperor, namely, Jesus of Nazareth. The confessions of faith call him the "King of the Jews," "King," the "King of Kings." To him belongs, as his disciples say, all power in heaven and on earth.

Blaise Pascal emphasized, as we have already mentioned, John 19:15 as the decisive words of the Jews in Je-

sus' trial. Now, toward the end of our study, we can more
clearly see why: *The trial of Jesus is a trial about the reign
of God.*

Jesus of Nazareth did not accidentally or incidental-
ly, but rather consciously, place the speech about God's
kingship, God's rule, and God's kingdom, at the heart of
his proclamation. He constantly and radically reminded his
listeners of the old principle of faith, that JHWH alone is
king and, as king of the world, has infused justice and righteousness into Israel and into the social life of the people.

The central concept of Jesus' proclamation is not
accidentally a socio-political, theologically precise concept,
namely, the kingship of God. Jesus, along with the tradition
of Israel, knows that JHWH, the only God, the creator of
the world, wants to be the king of a people who freely serve
him as their king and who thereby is a royal nation among
the nations of the world.

Within the context of an eschatological correction
of Israel's current watered-down theology, Jesus had proclaimed that God has initiated his kingly rule and that—as
far as he, God, is concerned—there is nothing more outstanding, so that Israel can become completely God's place
of dominion; outstanding is only the conversion of Israel
and trust in the joyful news of God's dominion.

Jesus himself had experienced himself as the first
eschatological "discoverer" of God's dominion and had
made his "discovery" known through his efforts to gather
Israel, in word and deed. In his rejection of the demonization of his ministry, he could say: "But if it is by the finger
of God that I cast out demons, then the kingdom of God has
come to you." God's kingdom proves to be redemptive for
Israel and for the world; for everyone who trusts in this
king.

The trial of Jesus is concerned with trust in this
king—with faith. Those who put their trust in other gods
and allow themselves to be ruled by the gods as demonic
idols, decide against Jesus.

"We have no king but the emperor." Thus John

characterizes the language of unbelief.

Unbelief betrays God and God's Messiah in favor of the representative of the world.

Pascal saw correctly that traitors unwillingly speak the truth: They have no king because they have rejected JHWH as their king; because they do not allow God's will, as revealed to them through the Messiah, to reign over them.

They have only the emperor as king because the emperor claims every person as his subject.

They betrayed their freedom.

The trial of Jesus is concerned with the messianic freedom which God's dominion establishes.

The emperor enslaves . . .

Jesus had said: "The kings of the Gentiles lord it over them, and their great men exercise authority over them. But it shall not be so among you." Jesus entrusted the community of his disciples within the renewed people of God with the freedom of service, with the courage to inaugurate the silent revolution.

"The ruler of this world has been condemned" (John 16:11)

Believers do not presuppose that unbelief will be victorious in this world and will reign over this world. The Johannine Jesus maintains that believers would experience, in the continuation of his trial and through his Advocate, the Paraclete, the Holy Spirit, that "the ruler of this world" is condemned.

The Paraclete, whom Jesus sends, "will prove the world wrong about sin and righteousness and judgment; about sin, because they do not believe in me; about righteousness, because I am going to the Father and you will see me no longer; about judgment, because the ruler of this world has been condemned" (John 16:8-11).

What is required of human beings, of Jews as well

as Gentiles, is the forming of an opinion about the advent, the ministry, and the history of Jesus of Nazareth. To form an opinion about Jesus is to form an opinion about him as the "initiator and perfector of faith," as the Letter to the Hebrews calls him, and, today, about the community of his followers in faith. Of course, unbelief in the church makes forming an opinion problematic.

Søren Kierkegaard identified this problem in his diaries in the following manner: "If we are truly Christians; if 'Christianity,' a 'Christian world,' is ordered on Christian principles, then the New Testament is no longer, and can no longer be, the guide for Christians. If things were not so: that our concept of a Christian is mere fancy; that the whole machinery of the state church and 1000 spiritual-worldly administrators is a huge deception which does not in the least help us in eternity, but which, just the opposite, will turn on us in accusation—if things were not so; for, in this case, we surely want to rid ourselves as quickly as possible of this machinery, for the sake of eternity. . . If things were not so, if the Christian really is what we understand one to be, then what is God in heaven? He is the most ridiculous being that ever lived; his word, the most ridiculous book ever discovered. To move heaven and earth (as he does in his word), to threaten with hell, with eternal punishment, in order to get what we understand a Christian to be (and we are surely genuine Christians!)—no, something so ridiculous has never before existed!" And Kierkegaard had only observed the state church at the beginning of the nineteenth century, not yet post-Holocaust Christianity at the end of the twentieth century.

What should the Advocate of Jesus, the Paraclete, the Holy Spirit, still accomplish "with respect to justice"? The evangelist believes that the justification of the Son, God's verdict about his trial, is the Son's going to the Father, his resurrection and exaltation. Yet this verdict remains for the church, prior to the Parousia, a believed, but not yet a revealed, verdict, which it, of course, can only further in its existence and praxis. And if it hides it?

Who should then be able to recognize that the Messiah in fact has already come in Jesus of Nazareth?

Even today a suffering because of God's people, in and with the church, is possible and necessary—as with Jesus himself. If we ask ourselves why Jesus was silent about so many things during his trial, we would have to answer: because his accusers did not want to hear the truth; because very rarely does anyone want to. The only thing that can draw attention to it is silence—particularly in the situation of an accused person.

Where the church is not persecuted, it has the chance—through a lived-out criticism, through nonconformity, through a new form of life—to give evidence for its truth. Francis of Assisi did this in his own way during his own time, to some degree by specifically renouncing preaching. He wanted to allow the kingdom of Christ to shine through his life and the lives of his disciples, as well as through their common life together.

And today? How does the church manifest Christ's kingdom? Did it not long ago make its peace with the "inherent laws" of many areas of life, to the so-called autonomy of the world? Has it not often allowed the "prince of this world" to reign in the church? He is not the Advocate of Jesus . . .

The prince of this world has already been sentenced because God stands on the side of Jesus; in the church, he must *experience* his condemnation.

The trial of Jesus continues—although the verdict has been pronounced.

The trial of Jesus continues—although the revision is complete.

The trial of Jesus continues—"because they do not believe in me."

EPILOGUE

Not long ago, in a "Versuch über die 'Shoah'" (Akzente 3/1987), George Steiner meditated on Paul Celan's *Psalm* and thereby considered the following:

"If, according to Christian belief, a divine being, a son of God and of man, died in the passion of Christ *for* human beings, then one could understand it thus: In the Shoah, the Jewish people ("root, matrix")—

> (root
> Abraham's root. Jesse's root.
> Nobody's
> root—o
> our.)—

died *for* God; they took upon themselves the unimaginable guilt of God's indifference or absence or powerlessness."

George Steiner remarks that such reflections are "inaccessible to rational analysis." He also leaves open the question, whether they are adequate for an understanding of the Shoah.

Is it meaningful or possible for us to follow his train of thought? Whom else should "the unimaginable guilt of God's indifference or absence or powerlessness" concern than Christians, who allowed God to appear, to degenerate, thus?

If the Jewish people died "*for* God" in the Shoah, then it seems that it took upon itself, in such a way, "the unimaginable guilt" of the non-people of a divided Christianity, whose members had promoted anti-Judaism and acted against the Jews in God's name.

Could the non-people, together with the people, become a single people of God in a new way?

The servant of God who died for human beings and the servant of God who died "for God"—do they not belong together, to each other?

Is not the hidden blossom of hope in Paul Celan's *Psalm* (see below)—trusting in Nobody—the new life coming from eternal pre-existence?

Did not Jesus of Nazareth become "nobody" for the Jewish people—as the Jews have become in our century for Christianity?

Can we possibly interpret Paul Celan's text by substituting Jews and Christians for "o our"—Abraham's root?

And could the "us" and "we" of the psalm mean both—in one people of the "Nobody's-rose"?

Must that which is impossible for rational analysis remain hidden from our sight? With the help of Paul Celan's *Psalm*, one may meditate on Jesus' trial . . .

PSALM

No one moulds us again out of earth and clay
no one conjures our dust.
No one.

Praise be to you, no one.
For you,
we would flower.
Toward you.

A nothing
were we, are we, shall
we remain, flowering:
The nothing—, the
No one's-rose.
With the stylus soul-bright,
the stamen heaven-ravaged,

the crown red
from the crimson word, which we sang
over, o over
the thorn.

(Paul Celan)

Crown, crimson, thorn—words of the passion
of Jesus.
His trial—his passion.
The witness: Whoever takes up his cross . . .